Anna Hought

ANNA

by

Anna Guttormsen Hought

with Florence Ekstrand

Welcome Press
Seattle, Washington

To Nora

ISBN 0-916871-09-6

Welcome Press
2701 Queen Anne Avenue N.
Seattle, WA 98109

Manufactured in the United States of America

Foreword

Much has been written about the immigrant women who elbowed their fearful way through teeming Ellis Island, who wept for the sound of their own tongue again, who found the new land to be something less than that of the legendary gold-paved streets.

More has been written about the homesteading women who struck out from their settled homes in New York State, Ohio, Kentucky, pushing west, braving blizzards, sod huts, Indians and lonely childbirth, their eyes finding no end to the prairie, their lives often isolated from all humans but their husbands and children.

But the life of Anna Guttormsen Hought is fascinating to us because she is both. Coming from her native Norway as a single woman of 29, she homesteaded alone on the windswept prairies of northern Montana.

More than that, she is here to tell about it — ninety-nine years old at this writing. She is a living link. Tucked away in a fertile, retentive mind, her stories of a Norwegian childhood and life on the prairie have been brought out time and again, first for her child Nora, then for grandchildren, then for friends and children of friends. Still handsome, still vibrant, with a dramatic flair, she reconstructs the dialogue of eighty and ninety years ago as if it were last week. Underlying the gentleness that is her nature is a sense of humor that comes near to being described as "rollicking."

The accounts in this book are almost exactly as Anna told them. Many are taken verbatim from her own writing in notebooks, scraps of paper, old calendar pages and the backs of writing tablets.

But when we had assembled most of them, something was wrong.

"Anna, almost all of your recollections are happy ones. What about the hard times?"

Anna shrugged. "Oh, you forget them."

"But what about leaving your parents, not knowing if you'd ever see them again?"

"It was hard, yes, but they thought I was doing the right thing. And so did I."

"But what about standing at your window and seeing nothing but prairie and a pump that drew alkali water? Didn't you dream of Drammen fjord and Skoger and Bakken, where your cousins lived and had a brook running through their yard?"

"I suppose I did. But this was my home, and I wanted to make things nice, first for myself, and then for my husband and little girl."

"But you came from a good job in Oslo, you had friends your own age, an active social life, a bustling city. And you found cowboys and farmers' wives with a language that wasn't always familiar, and your social life was programs at a one-room school and visits with a neighbor when you could get away from all that work."

"But we were helping each other, and we were

making things fun. And," she added emphatically, "they were fun!"

Finally, after some gentle prodding on the part of Anna's daughter Nora, we came to know more about the difficult times: the heart ailment that plagued and hampered Anna from the time of Nora's birth until well into her fifties; the pain of losing little Mary Elaine, her second child, at the age of three months; the letter that came many months late telling of her mother's death in Norway; the heartbreak of always hoping for a better crop year and seeing the dreams die on a dry prairie; the final blow during the drought of the 1930s, when families in droves walked away from their farms.

What gives us that remarkable bent for blotting out pain and remembering delight? For Anna, it was no Pollyanna outlook born of an unreasoning faith. A deep religious faith had been hers from childhood, but few pastors came the thirty-five miles from Malta to comfort and exhort. "We never talked much about faith in God," Nora recalls, "but we knew it was there."

Is there, perhaps, as some believe, a biological mischief that makes some of us complainers and others survivors? Is it rooted in Viking blood, in seafarers and fishermen along the rocky coasts? Can it be learned? Absorbed?

The Norwegian character has often been called "stoic." But "stoic" implies facing hardship with a certain grimness, accepting without flinching. Anna adds another dimension, that of confronting difficulties and turning them into something good. This ability no doubt had its roots in a stable childhood filled with love. A sense of adventure, fostered by life near the sea, stood her in good stead. The years of young womanhood in Oslo, a city awakening to Norway's new national freedom, must have been years of shaping values. So she had inner resources to draw on when, at 29, she jolted in a hay wagon over thirty-five miles of rain-rutted road, when she saw what she thought was a chicken coop but was in truth her home, and when she looked life in the face and began, as she put it so many times, "to make things nice."

There is a book, translated from the Norwegian, about another Anna, Anna of Haugsetvolden in Solendalen on Lake Ister. In an afterword to that book, Siegfried Lenz writes,
"Wherever men suffer poverty and fight hardship, wherever one of us finds a last resort to meet the challenges of existence, there is an example, a model: we confront the center of being. Which is why after reading Anna's life story we know more about ourselves."

This is no less true of Anna Guttormsen Hought.

Skoger: A Norwegian Childhood

For Norway the latter half of the 19th century was a time of awakening, of stretching. After centuries of domination by first Denmark, then Sweden, movements were afoot to build a national solidarity, movements that would culminate in achieving complete independence from Sweden.

Social change as much as political was involved as Norwegians struggled to create unity between rural peasants (some of whom owned land and were fairly well-to-do) and what had always been the "privileged class." The meeting ground came to be, in large part, the old folk ways.

Americans — and even the British — do not always understand the impact of folk songs, folk dances, folk museums, folk dress. But, as historian T.K. Derry puts it, "on the continent an almost mystical significance has been attached to the evidences of a past way of living." During the later decades of 1800 the tales of Asbjørnsen and Moe, couched in the language of the rural, ordinary people, wakened a pride in being "the common man." Historian P.A. Munch, musicians Ole Bull and Edvard Grieg, and writers like

B.A. Bjørnson, A.O. Vinje, and others carried the torch. Henrik Ibsen, by contrast, decried the romantic backward look at the past, but his own controversial ideas sparked perhaps the greatest excitement of all. Norwegians were becoming joyfully aware of themselves as a people.

On June 7, 1905, the Norwegian Storting passed and sent to the Swedish king a resolution stating that "the union between Sweden and Norway under the same king is dissolved and the king has ceased to function as king of Norway." A period of crisis lasted through that summer and into the fall, but on October 26, 1905, King Oscar renounced the Norwegian throne. In November, the people voted to endorse the choice of Danish Prince Charles, who took as his Norwegian name King Haakon VII.

The years immediately following were like a national idyll. Norway became the most advanced sovereign state in Europe. Suffrage was granted to women. Farming techniques improved; farmers began buying goods being produced. Industrial wage earners experienced better times. As early as 1886, women operators worked in a modern telephone exchange in Oslo. The use of hydroelectricity was changing the country's economic life. And when Norway marked the 100th anniversary of her constitution (granted by Denmark in 1814) with a big centennial exposition in Oslo, Norwegians looked back on a century of slow progress and burgeoning national pride.

It was into such a background that Anna Guttormsen was born in 1887 and here she grew to young womanhood.

*   *   *

The big, dark woods that lay between my cousins' house and my home was full of frightening things. But up in the woods above our place was a patch where we loved to play. It was here I persuaded my two older brothers to build a playhouse for me. George and John nailed boards from tree to tree and wove evergreen branches between them to form walls. There was an opening for a door and even a window. I could stand and see my own house through the trees. A big chunk of wood made the table and smaller ones were chairs.

Sunday came, a day to have company. I invited my mother and father for after-dinner coffee.

"Yes, but we must have our nap first," said Father.

"And will you please bring the coffee with you?"

"Do you have anything to go with the coffee?"

"No, so maybe you could bring a few cookies."

I laid the table with a small cloth and my toy coffee service and waited. How long it took them to nap!

Then I saw them walking up through the trees. The copper coffee pot glinted in the sun that came through the leaves. Mother carried a big plate of sandwiches and cookies. Father said grace before I poured the coffee. George and John joined in, but when the sandwiches were gone, so were they! We chatted in a most grown-up manner. When Father and Mother rose to leave, both shook my hand and said, "Tack før maten," which means "Thank you for the food," and I replied, "Velbekomme," or "You're welcome."

Why is this memory so vivid? Was it the sense of having my own four walls, a special place that was my very own? Or was it the warm love of parents who humored a little girl by giving up a Sunday afternoon to treat her as an equal? The memory would lend me

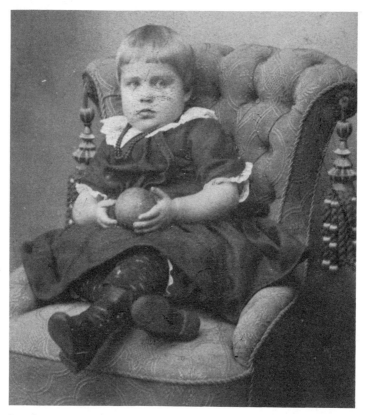

Anna Guttormsen at two.

strength in years to come when my parents were but a memory and my four walls were a shack on a wind-swept prairie.

How much a part of my life were those woods! Some of my earliest memories are of my mother and my two older brothers going up into the woods to gather kindling for the kitchen fire. Often I would walk along behind them, gathering wild flowers, chattering to the imaginary playmate who always walked beside me, listening to the birds. Sometimes I went off alone into the woods gathering small twigs and making "kindling piles" like the others.

After a while Mother would realize I was gone. But she could always find me by following the trail of little piles of twigs on the forest floor. Sometimes she would find me asleep under a tree. She never scolded. Instead she'd say, "Come, I have a nice little surprise for you at home," and she'd put me on her back and carry me home. So there were two adventures—the walk into the forest and the surprise at home. It might be a bowl of *søtsuppe* (fruit soup) she had just made or waffles with raspberry jam.

But peaceful as our small area was, it could be full of terrors, too. The trees and rocky outcroppings seemed to draw lightning storms. Thunder clouds could roll over the hills or move quickly across Drammen fjord. I was so terrified of thunder that if it caught me outside I would stand frozen to the spot. One summer day I dressed up in Mother's long black skirt, pinned my hair into a pug and walked down our road, chatting with myself as if I were two people. A sudden, unexpected shower drenched me and on top of that came thunder and lightning. All I could think of was to grab the fence by the side of the road to steady myself. It was the worst place I could have been. But Mother was watching from the house and she came running. She scooped me up and brought me to the house.

Mother's touch was gentle, but there was little that escaped her eye.

From the time that I was very small I had to wash the dishes. I hated it and more than once I managed to hide some of the soiled plates or pans. Mother was wise to my tricks. She would find the unwashed dishes and ever so nicely bring them back to me, saying, "Here, you almost forgot these."

One day she trusted me to wash her beautiful gold-rimmed cup. I took it by the handle, wadded the whole dishcloth into the cup, pushed and pulled it. Suddenly, there I was with the handle in one hand and the cup in the other—and I was scared to death!

"Mamma," I cried, "I couldn't help it! I couldn't help it!"

Mother took it and stood looking at it with an absent expression. "My beautiful cup that I got at my wedding," she murmured under her breath, all the while trying to fit the handle back on the cup.

I wished she would spank me. It wouldn't have hurt nearly as much as standing there and seeing her lost in memories about that cup.

Potatoes were our staple food and they were kept in the cellar. Often I was sent down to bring up some potatoes for dinner. One day when Mother was in a particular hurry, I managed to dawdle about the cellar until I found myself in the corner where the jams and jellies were kept. They were put up in large stone crocks, but I knew what they were for the jam crocks were always covered with a particular kind of paper and tied with a string.

I knew how good and sweet the contents of those crocks were and how much I longed for a taste. Then—miracle of miracles—the paper came off one. There lay the raspberry jam. But I had no spoon, so I dipped my hand into the jam and scooped a large paw-full into my mouth.

From upstairs came Mother's voice. "Anna, what's taking you so long? You aren't in the jam, are you?"

"Oh, no!" I swallowed frantically.

"Well, hurry now, bring the potatoes."

Upstairs, Mother took the potatoes and set them on the table. Then she picked me up and held me in front of the mirror that hung by the washstand. My face was so covered with jam that I caught my breath, frightened. Now I was really in for it!

But Mother said, "Anna, Jesus saw what you did down there and it hurt Him."

How could He see in the cellar? It was so dark

down there that I could barely see my way myself!

"And you lied, and that made Him feel bad. And it made me feel bad to think that I had a girl who lied."

There was no spanking, but bit by bit I was beginning to know right from wrong.

But sometimes even my parents' patience was exhausted.

It was midsummer, a glorious time in Norway. The days were very long. Flowers were in bloom in the forest. Wild strawberries were red; they were small but sweet as sugar. Maybe even our family cow was giddy with the season for she failed to come home for milking one night and brother John and I were sent to fetch her.

But John and I found something more exciting than the cow—a patch of wild strawberries. The cow was forgotten. John and I kept picking. First we ate. Then we filled John's cap. Then we threaded the small, firm berries on straws until we had almost more than we could handle. Only then did we realize the cow was nowhere to be seen and we had been there for a long, long time.

It was still dusk when we reached home. But the door was locked. Worried, we pounded on it.

"You've been out this long," called Father, "you can stay out the rest of the night."

"No, please, let me come in!" I cried. "Mamma, let me in!"

"Allright for them," muttered John. "They won't get any of my berries. I'm going to the barn to sleep in the haymow."

"I'll still give Mamma my berries," I called after him. I saw the barn door close behind him. I was alone. In the strange half-lit night everything was so quiet, so eerie. I began to cry. At last I was let in. It turned out that the cow had come home by herself, was milked and put in the barn for the night. Another lesson was impressed on me: when there's a chore to be done, it's best not to get side-tracked.

It was a small world, our world at Skoger. Far, far back I remember the sound of apples falling off the tree on a Sunday morning, hitting the roof and rolling down the slope to the ground. I remember going out in my nightgown and bringing in as many as I could carry, and the three of us lay in bed eating juicy, crackling apples until Mother got up and made coffee.

Skoger, the area where we lived, lay outside the town of Drammen. We could look out on Drammen fjord.

My father, Ole Guttormsen, had been born in Rukkedalen, Nes, Hallingdal, on October 1, 1855. His parents were Guttorm and Anna Lokken. When he was a young man, he came to Drammen to look for work. Here he met my mother, Joanna Jensen, who had been born March 12, 1862, in Bakken, Skoger. Her parents were Jens and Marie Jensen.

Grandfather Jensen was a foreman at the glass factory, Glasverket, in Drammen. Grandmother baked and sold bread which, I was later told by many, was out of this world. Besides my mother, they had six other children. To ease the burden of supporting so many children, three sons left home. Hans went to Honolulu and Masilius (Maas) to Queensland, Australia. Both married in their respective new settlements and raised families. Thorvald went to sea; he was drowned when his ship went down in a terrible storm. Otto remained at home. Then there were Tante (Aunt) Lina, Tante Martine, and my mother Joanna, called "Janna" for short.

In my immediate family, my brother George was born April 5, 1881, and my brother John on January 25, 1883, both in Skoger, Drammen. I was born

The public square in Drammen.

April 29, 1887, also in Skoger. I was named for my two grandmothers, Anna Marie. And I remember well when my little brother Oscar was born, on August 9, 1893, when I was six. How I loved my little brother! I spent many hours trying to teach him to walk. I would dress him in my little dresses that were too small for me. One day I dressed him in a particularly fine dress, a red one with black dots, and took him walking down the road to show him off. A nice couple from town came by in a carriage and I curtsied to them — and so did Oscar. They stopped.

"And what is your name, little girl?" asked the man.

"Anna Marie," I replied.

"And yours?" he asked Oscar.

"Oscar Marie," came the reply.

I hurried to explain to the puzzled pair that he really was a boy.

Our home was a small place with a few acres of

land. We usually had one or two cows, a few pigs, some chickens and a large garden. I had a small garden of my own under an apple tree and learned to know the difference between weeds and vegetables and flowers. Father worked as an overseer over the workers on a large farm.

The kitchen was long and narrow, with a fireplace in one corner. It was an open fireplace and at first Mother did all her cooking over that fire. Then we got a cast-iron stove with two lids, and finally one with four lids—what luxury. Under the windows was built a cupboard with a work top and drawers for tableware and utensils. At the end stood two enamel pails with a dipper. We had a lovely cold spring not far from the house and it was up to us children to carry the water. I could only manage one pail at a time but the boys would bring two. When Father came home from work, especially after a long, hot day, we had to make sure there was fresh, cold water in the pails. This was especially true in August when the corn was ripening. (In Norway all grain was called "corn"—rye, barley, all grains used for feed.)

In the living room, which was also a bedroom, were a large double bed and a sofa that opened up into a bed, called a "commerce," where I slept. Off the kitchen was a large bedroom for the boys and also two small rooms for storage, one for good clothes and the other for work clothes. These were not finished but cozy. Stairs led from the large hall up to one large room with a bed in it. Sometimes our cousins Ragna and Guri would come and stay a spell and they would sleep there.

Not far from our house, in an area called Petters Lokka, was an enormous flat rock, for there were many outcroppings of rock in the woods and hills. Here we and our cousins and other children in the neighborhood would gather to dance and play games, and to swing in a rope swing in a nearby tree.

Also in the deep woods I would go to gather pine cones for a quick, hot fire on the day my mother ironed clothes. The "bolts" or heavy irons that fitted inside an iron case with a handle, were heated in the open fire. It was my job to exchange the bolts when they cooled. I would use a long tong to handle them. When the iron Mother was using grew cool, I would lift the red-hot bolt from the fire and slip it in, putting the cooled one back into the fire. Years later, in my prairie shack, I ironed in a similar way, with irons heated on the stove.

In spite of all the chores that had to be done, my childhood memories are happy ones. My earliest ones are twined with memories of Aase, my doll, and Mimi, the cat. Mimi was more person than cat. She had been born on my birthday and someone gave her to John, who brought her home to us. Whenever any one of us left to walk to the village or to our cousins', she would follow us part way down the road. There she would sit and wait until we came back. As soon as she saw us coming, she'd meow and hurry to follow us back to the house. (The day John left for America, Mimi disappeared; she was never found.)

Aase was a precious doll. She was perhaps twelve inches long, with a cloth body and china head. From the time I was big enough to thread a needle, Mother would give me scraps of cloth and I would sew clothes for Aase.

There was one day when I was sitting in one of the apple trees in our yard, playing with Aase. From where I sat I could see Mother and the boys moving about in the kitchen. (And, adventurous child that I was, I'm sure she was glad to have me where she could keep an eye on me, too.) One of our cows, Jomfru Coll, had been turned loose to graze in the yard. She was careful to stay away from the clotheslines, which

Mother had that day stretched back and forth between the apple trees and on which the washing now hung. Soon Jomfru was nibbling the green grass under the tree in which I sat. I looked down at her. What a lovely cow she was, no horns and with a bell that jangled softly as she moved her head back and forth. What a nice, broad back she had! What fun it would be to take a horseback ride on that back!

It was no sooner said than done, and I was on Jomfru's back. The startled cow jerked her head up and began to run. Her bell jangled wildly. Out of the corner of my eye I caught sight of Mother, George and John in the window. They were laughing, but not for long.

Suddenly the cow made a dive under the clotheslines. The line caught me squarely under the chin, dumping me off. Mother and the boys came running and carried me in to bed, where I stayed for three days. My throat was so bruised I couldn't eat or drink or talk for all that time. No one even thought of calling a doctor, because we made no use of doctors in that time unless someone was seriously ill. There were deaconesses who came and helped at childbirth; we had great respect for them and they were considered to be next to a doctor. But somehow we made it through childhood without much help from either.

I was an adventurous child, yes, but some of the things I did must have been almost foolhardy. Once, when I was about six, I was looking out at the road when I saw a team and wagon come racing down the road. The driver must have been thrown out for the runaway team was without a driver. I don't know what I was thinking—maybe I was afraid for children down the road—but I ran out into the road and stood right in the middle of it with my arms stretched out. The horses came full speed toward me but I stood my ground. They ground to a stop right in front of me, snorting and blowing through their big nostrils. I was trembling, but I stood there until the driver came and picked up the lines. He got into what was left of the wagon and drove off.

Being so near Drammen fjord was an invitation to adventure. Once we went swimming in Drammen's elv-fjord and while we were in someone stole our clothes. We were left naked and shivering until a friend rescued us. Once John almost drowned in the same part of the fjord. He had gone down twice and was about to go down a third time when someone managed to get hold of him.

And one spring day when the ice was breaking up along the shore, we decided to go fishing off the ice floes. We stepped and jumped from one ice chunk to another, fish poles in hand, until a man shouted from shore,

"Get back to shore right away or you'll drown! Those ice floes are moving further out!"

We hopped from one to another, working our way to shore, and as we did we could hear the ice cracking beneath us. Poor mothers! No wonder they turn gray before their time.

Going to play with my cousins was an adventure in itself. There were eight of them. Their little cottage was on a hillside and was appropriately called "Bakken," which means "the hill." It looked out on a beautiful view of Drammen fjord, and always the Norwegian flag flew in the wind. In front of the cottage was a great, old cherry tree and all who came were welcome to pick and eat when the fruit was on.

Tante Lina was my mother's sister. Uncle Carl was foreman at the Drammen Jernstropperi (ironworks). Grandfather Jensen made his home with them, all good Christian people who loved the Lord. The children were Johann, Ragna, Conrad, Lizzie,

Matilda, Sigurd, Martin, Alf, and Jennie.

Staying with the cousins was particularly fun because Grandfather had built his own coffin and kept it in an upstairs room. It was a fine, long pine box and he had painted it black both inside and out. Since Grandfather was not ready for it yet, we children found it a fine place in which to play.

Finally came the day when I was old enough to stay overnight with cousin Lizzie. What a grownup feeling! I must have been five. I went early in the day to have plenty of time to play. There was a tiny brook that bubbled down from the woods and into the yard at Bakken. At the point where it ran into the fenced yard was a little bridge. Here Lizzie and I lay on our stomachs and watched the water hurry through. Sometimes a leaf came floating by, sometimes we just lay and looked at our reflections in the water.

Tante Lina came out of the house. "You children mustn't put anything in there," she called. "That's our drinking water."

"No, Tante," I replied, "*vi bare speile oss* (we are just using it as a mirror!)"

"Ja, then you'd better come in and I'll give you something good," called Tante.

It didn't take us long. The "something good" turned out to be a big slice of home-baked bread with sugar on it, a treat for us children who seldom had candy. (I will say I fared better than some of the others. There was an old man who sometimes walked to town past our place. Many of the children teased him, but I was polite and kind to him and he would usually give me a little bag of candy on his way home.)

All went well that day until dusk began to creep over the hillside. Suddenly the thought of my own bed at home was more than I could bear. I picked up my nightgown, said goodnight to Tante Lina and started for the door.

"But, Anna, you were going to stay all night this time."

"No, I think I'd better go home before it gets dark."

But going home in the long dusk took all the courage I had. It meant first going through a small wooded pasture where several horses were loose and always very curious about anyone who walked through there. They would follow us, nip at our clothes and blow through their big nostrils.

Further along in the woods was an old black-smith shop, almost lost in the bushes that had grown up around it. It was dark and spooky, for the man who had owned it had died in there while working. That was always enough to frighten us children. The door hung open and it would swing in the wind, making strange creaking sounds. That night the noises were more frightening than ever and I ran until I finally reached the road. Then there was another half mile to go, and I ran that as fast as I could. Finally I burst into the house.

"The horses were after me," I panted, "and I saw *spøkery*!" I needed help to get to bed that night. Actually it was hard to help a child to get over being afraid of ghosts, for I noticed whenever grownups got together, especially the men, there was a good deal of talk about "spooks" and other-worldly creatures.

Just as chores started early for children, so we learned to do handwork at an early age, although I never learned a great deal of stitchery. I remember a little bag I knitted, about five inches square, with two holes where I dropped stitches. But most of all I remember the *sukker og fløte* doily.

In a store window I had seen a doily stamped with the words *sukker og fløte*, which means "sugar and cream." I wanted to buy it and embroider it for my mother for her birthday. But it cost twenty-five cents, and I had no money. And since it was to be a surprise, I wouldn't ask her for money.

Two women in Drammen owned a small bakery with two little tables in front where one could have a cup of coffee and perhaps some sweets from the bakery. Surely they would want some flowers for their tables.

Blåveis are a small blue flower that grow so early in the spring that they bloom under the snow. One must scrape off the snow to pick them. I gathered a big handful of them and brought them to the bakery and showed them to the proprietors.

"Oh, look," cried one of the women, "a whole bouquet of *blåveis!*"

"They're for sale," I said, "for twenty-five cents."

"Here," said one of the women, "here are three nice cookies for your flowers."

It was hard to turn down those cookies, but I took my flowers and marched out the door. I walked to a big house on another street, the home of Consul Gram, the richest man in town. A big wooden fence ran all the way around the yard and seven black and white hunting dogs barked in the back yard. I rang the bell and when the hired girl opened the door I said, "I would like to see Fru Gram."

She brought me through the house to the kitchen, where the cook, the *barnepike* (nursemaid) and another maid or two were busy. Soon I heard a rustle of silk coming down the hall. It was Fru Gram.

"Oh, look at the beautiful flowers."

"They are for sale."

"How much?"

"Twenty-five cents."

"Oh, of course. I will go get the money. Here," she called to the hired girl, "put the flowers on the dining room table and set another place. This little girl will eat breakfast with us."

So she bought the flowers and I ate breakfast in the enormous dining room, thinking all the while about the hole in the elbow of my sweater.

But the consul and his wife put me at ease, and the consul reminded me that his sons had taken my brothers hunting with them.

So I bought the *sukker og fløte* doily and embroidered it for my mother as a surprise. To make the scalloped edge, I used a thimble for a pattern. I drew the tiny scallops all around, then finished them with a satin stitch and cut them out. I was six or seven at the time.

I was about fifteen when I made a Hardanger-embroidered tablecloth for my mother, again as a surprise. This time I had to count threads in the material, cut out and weave in the open spaces. Years later, when I first came to America, my mother sent me a large piece of Hardanger to work. "See how much you can do before you come to Norway again," she wrote. Well, I knew what she was thinking—she didn't want me running around. I finished that one and I'm not sure how many more, and when I was in my nineties I found myself teaching classes in the craft.

Another embroidery I learned was *bondesøm*, a solid stitch done in bright colors. People in the mountains loved bright colors, which is where it got its name.

The summer I was seven, I went with my father on a very strange journey. Strange and sad and happy. All I knew was that I was going with Father to Hallingdal and I had a new straw hat with ribbons hanging down the back, and a nice small suitcase.

One summer morning we started out by train. We crossed over Krødern, a small inland lake, in a small boat called the *Bøya*. From there we had *skyss*, meaning a long trip by hired horse, buggy, and driver.

When we came to Nes, there was a family related to Father's farm owner in Drammen and we stayed over-night with them.

In the morning their horse and buggy took us a way on our road, to Rukkedalen. From here we walked perhaps a couple of miles. We were growing hungry and thirsty, and we stopped at a farm where the wife gave us cheese sandwiches; Father had coffee and I had milk. I remember I had to wash the mold off the cheese, and I wondered if the water was clean. I realized not everyone was as particular about cleanli-ness as Mamma.

After a little rest we started out again, climbing gradually uphill. Soon I was tired and hungry again.

"Do we eat now?" I asked again and again.

"When we come to the right place," replied Father.

In time we came to a little red house with white shutters and a white picket fence around the spotless yard. Through the window I could see a lady spin-ning. She was small, with black hair pulled tightly back. She was watching us as we approached.

"Shall we go in and ask if we can have something to eat?"

Father nodded. When the little lady opened the door, Father asked, "Could we buy a little food?"

"*Ja da*," she replied. "You must be from town then?"

"Yes, from Drammen."

"*Nej, oh nej*. I have a son there. He went to Dram-men when he was only sixteen."

By this time I was already in the house. It was like a doll house. I thought it was beautiful. Everything was decorated with rosemaling—the wide door frames, around the windows, the *høy sete*, a bench with a high back. There was a high bed in the room, so high that there were steps going up to it, with rose-maling on every step. I was so fascinated I began climbing the steps while they talked. Suddenly on a shelf I spied two familiar pictures.

"That's me," I cried, pointing to the first picture. And, "That's Mamma, too!"

Then I saw that Father was crying, and the small lady with black hair was wiping her eyes with the corner of her big apron.

I went outside and played with the lambs in the yard. Just across the road, a larger house with several outbuildings sat on the edge of a ravine that dropped sharply downward. I sat and wondered what would happen if a wind blew it over the edge.

I was to learn later that many years before, as a young man, Father had come to Drammen from Hallingdal. A former neighbor and friend had moved to Drammen and bought a farm, and at sixteen Father had found work on that farm. He had never been back to Hallingdal. I am not sure, but I think that father's half-brother was their mother's favorite and was getting the farm. Father pulled out and left the farm to his half-brother and never went back.

How many times I have wondered about that day. Why hadn't Father told me we were going to visit his mother, my *farmor*? Could it be that the blame had been his, that he wanted to be sure we were welcome before he told me who this little lady was who wiped her eyes on her apron?

Soon my grandmother called me to come in and eat. Now there was a huge goat cheese on the table, and everything was happy. Father and Grandmother talked and talked.

We stayed two weeks. The big house across the road was the house where Grandmother had raised her children. Now it belonged to Father's half-brother, but apparently no hard feelings remained. In the house was a huge fireplace. It burned big logs, and many nights we gathered around it. Others came to visit. Some of the old people still wore the folk costume of the area. (The younger ones did only if it was a very special occasion.) We children sat wide-eyed and listened to the men tell ghost stories.

"Per Spellman," said Father, "sat right on that bridge and played his violin, just the way he used to play at dances. He fell backward and broke his neck. But he sits there at the bridge yet and plays his violin. You can hear him . . . ."

The children in the family and in the neighborhood were fascinated with my new straw hat. They all wore scarves tied under their chins. But my hat was of natural straw, with a wide brim. The ribbons down the back were long and shiny. There was an elastic to go under my chin. I wore it over my long blonde braids.

But while I was there I had to wear a scarf tied under my chin because the other girls all wanted to take turns wearing my hat.

When it was time to go, Father said, "Anna, leave your hat with the children."

"No, Father, for I have hardly worn it at all!"

"You aren't selfish, are you, Anna?"

"No, but . . . ." There was no way I could leave that beautiful hat behind!

So I wore it as we made the long walk and the buggy rides back to Krødern. When we got into the boat to cross the lake, the waves were choppy. The wind was brisk. Suddenly a gust caught my hat and sent it sailing into the choppy waves.

I can still feel the pain of standing there and watching that beautiful hat bob away on the water, its ribbons stretched out behind it.

All Father said was, "You could have left your hat."

Mother was standing by the fence looking out over Drammen fjord when we came up the road toward home. I set my suitcase down and went running to her.

"Oh, you're the nicest looking lady I've seen the

whole time!" I cried.

"Oh, now, that's no way to talk!"

"And, Mamma, they don't wash clothes like you do."

Father had caught up with us. "Now, Anna, you shouldn't criticize."

"But they don't," I insisted. "They roll the clothes on the board. Mamma scrubs them back and forth. She gets them cleaner."

That was my visit to my Grandmother Lokken. I loved it!

I started school in the spring, not fall. I had been waiting for weeks. Mother finally began to tell me, "When the peonies open in bloom, then you will start school." One day I picked one of the fat buds and broke it open. I took it to Mother.

"Now can I start school?"

When the day finally came, my brother John took me with him. The school for Grades 1 through 3 was right next door to the Drammen Glasverk. All three grades were in one large room with a woman teacher. When we reached fourth grade we went on to another school with a man teacher.

That first day there were many small ones starting school. John came in and sat with me for a while. When he figured I had settled down, he got up to leave to go on to his own school. But when he did, I gathered up my things and marched out after him.

The second day I had to walk to school alone. Mother had tears in her eyes as she told me goodbye. It was a long walk, first through a small woods, then through a little settlement, over a small creek, and up a hill.

When I got to the upper school I went to school on skis in winter. The wall of the school would be full of skis lined up side by side. In that school I went only

Anna (fourth row, second from left) in her school photo.

every other day, but for long hours. Different children
came here, too, than to the beginners' school.

Skis were so much a part of our life in winter. At
first I had only barrel staves that I went sliding along
on. How I envied John, who had his own skis and was
such an excellent skier that he won many ski competi-
tions. His skis were so beautiful! One day I borrowed
them without his permission. I wanted so badly to go
down this one steep hill on "real" skis. But halfway
down a man crossed in front of me and I hit him. All I
could think was, "The skis! The skis!" I walked into
the house that afternoon carrying the tip of one ski in
my hand and saying over and over, "I know I shouldn't
have done it, I know I shouldn't have done it."

On that same hill the boys in the neighborhood
built a jump-off, which we called the *hop.* I loved to be
up there but since I had no skis at the time I found
other things to do. I made a round dome of wet snowballs, putting them in rings like the tiers on a Norwegian wedding cake, or *kransekake.* I left spaces between the snowballs, then in the center I placed a

large lighted candle. The light sparkled out through all the little openings in the rows of snowballs. All over the valley people were saying, "What is that up on the *hop?*"

I was happy to be in school but I suppose my happiest memories are of summer vacations. Then came the long days of sunshine and warmth. And the flowers. There were not only the wild flowers to be gathered in the woods, but also the flowers that Mother grew. She raised flowers inside and outside, and made arrangements for funerals and other occasions. There were *jorgener, portulakk, lilje konval, nykkelblomst, kallaliljer.* And we had bleeding hearts, fuschias, asters and peonies of many shades.

But I'm sure my favorite flowers were those on the huge lilac bush that grew right beside the pigs' house.

I must tell you that our pigs were very special. They were white, and every week Mother washed them with soap and water and a brush. They kept themselves very clean, too, not at all the way we think of pigs. They had a place to sleep and another place for their toilet. We changed the straw in their sleeping place every week and they never soiled the straw. They were so smart. In fact, Father loved the pigs so much he refused to be around the place when the butcher came in December to slaughter two of them for Christmas and for winter food.

I loved them, too. I could lie for hours on top of the pighouse roof, under the big lilac bush, watching their every move. Sometimes when Mother came to feed the pigs she would find me up there asleep. They were well-fed pigs. Besides the corn and grain they were fed, Mother made them a special mash every baking day. While she was making bread, I was sent out to strip the leaves off nettles along fence lines and in the woods. Other leaves may have been gathered, too, and the boys may have picked out a bunch of small potatoes from the bin or from the patch. All of this was thrown into a heavy pot with water. Before the baking, the coals which had been heating up the huge oven were pulled out of the oven and placed in a corner of the hearth. Over them was placed this kettle to simmer. Enough flour was added to make it a good mash and, when it was cooled, the pigs loved it.

So it was a sad task for me at butchering time to have to stir the blood that was drained from the pig after it was stuck and before the meat-cutting began. It had to be stirred to keep it from lumping. I suppose the only thing that made it easier was the thought of blood sausage, blood *klub*, blood pancakes, *pølse*, and blood pudding coming up.

The two pigs butchered before Christmas saw us through a good part of the year. Together with bread, potatoes and cheese, they formed a staple of our diet. Mother made sausage and head cheese. Fried pork was packed down in huge crocks and covered with lard. It kept well. We also butchered a young steer or an old cow in the winter.

But Mother wanted us to have greens, and in summer many were available. Her garden had cabbage, beets, carrots, lettuce and onions in it. I was often sent out to pick wild caraway for greens. We put the chopped green part in cooked meats, as in cooking a soup bone. We even cut off the root part, sliced it fine and cooked it in soup along with small dumplings and maybe some barley. I was often sent out to snip off some parsley or grass onions (chives) which might be used in eggs or other dishes.

Summer of course brought wild blueberries for the picking. There were also wild strawberries and wild raspberries. There were apples and cherries for pie; I loved the wild taste of the cherries. Rognebær, the berries of the mountain ash, were good for jelly after they had been frosted a little. We had plum trees and gooseberries grew big below the pighouse.

We had our own milk and made our own cheese and butter, and we had whipping cream for desserts. We had eggs from our own chickens.

But bread was a big part of our diet, and Mother baked twenty-four loaves at a time. The flour was a mix of rye and wheat, ground at the mill from our own grain. Mother had a big *nuv*, a long, deep wooden tray with handles at both ends. In this she mixed the bread. The flour was laid in it, then the sugar and yeast added with the liquids. It took much, much mixing and kneading. When it was all kneaded smooth, she patted it and left it to rise. When it had raised, she formed the loaves and left them on boards to rise.

The big brick oven was in a shed behind the house. It had a heavy iron door, and in it we built a good fire with big chunks of wood. I wasn't very old before I learned to test the heat of the oven by sticking my hand inside it. The heat could be regulated by taking out a brick here and there or by putting some back in.

When the heat was right, I would run up into the woods to get some pine branches. These would be wired to a long stick, making a broom with which we swept out the coals that had formed. These were the coals we put in the fireplace hearth and it was over these that the big kettle of pig mash was cooked.

The loaves had been rising on two long boards, a dozen to a board. Now we took a long-handled wood utensil that had a thin, square piece of wood at the end, large enough to hold two loaves. We would put two loaves on it, push them into the oven, give the stick a quick push and the loaves would settle in to be baked.

It was my job to run out to the shed at intervals to see if the bread was ready. How I learned to tell that when I was so small I don't know. "Is the bread ready?" Mother would call. And I would answer "Yes," and we would use the long-handled "scoop" to bring the loaves out of the big oven.

This was our everyday bread. It was good tasting, satisfying, and nourishing.

But if there was one time of the year when we had foods that were very special, it was at Christmas time. Mother had a word for it then: *Ach mej!* It was an expression of great satisfaction. "*Ach mej!* Doesn't that cake look fine?"

Preparations for Christmas started early. We began to feel the excitement when Mother began cleaning house. Everything had to be scrubbed, including the plain wooden chairs with their many rungs. The curtains were all washed, starched, and ironed. They smelled so fresh and good! Mother thought it was important that everything smell fresh and clean.

We baked every kind of little cookies, or *småkaker — fattigmand, berliner kranser, sirupskaka* (molasses cookies). None were eaten before Christmas. We even baked little cookies for Mimi, the cat, and hung them low on the tree.

The boys went up into the woods to cut a Christmas tree for us. Sometimes, if the snow wasn't too deep, I could go along. We trimmed the tree with lots of cookies, woven paper baskets filled with candy and nuts and with our names on them, paper stars and tinsel and rope.

But the candles on the tree were not to be lighted until after our Christmas Eve supper. That evening we started with rømmegrøt, a rich milk, cream and flour pudding, like a soup course. After that came pork ribs and potatoes. We always had a rice pudding with an almond hidden in it; the one who got the nut would be the next one married.

There was never much in the way of gifts and the

gifts we did get were usually very practical. But the year that Oscar was five he got a toboggan. He was so excited that he sat on it all evening and no one could get him off it. I got an apron that same year and my brother John liked it so well he wore it all evening. It was at Christmas I gave my mother the *sukker og fløte* doily. And the year I was fifteen I started to make her a Hardanger-embroidered tablecloth a yard square. It was for the table in the living room, over which hung a lamp that pulled up and down, with prisms around it and room for three candles, each with prisms underneath. The cloth (which got finished just in time for Mother's birthday in May) was laid over a plush tablecloth with fringes, and a plant was set in the middle.

One year when I was quite small, I had seen a miniature mask made of marzipan candy in a shop window. I was fascinated by it. How I wanted that tiny mask! It cost perhaps twenty-five cents, but I didn't have the money. So I begged Mother to give me the marzipan mask for Christmas.

"You have plenty," said Mother. But I begged (I might say "pestered") her until she gave in and gave me twenty-five cents. I ran to the store and bought the candy mask. I brought it home and it was hung on the Christmas tree, which we were not allowed to see until Christmas Eve.

Meanwhile, Mother and Father had invited guests for Christmas Eve. Down the road a way lived a woman who worked in the brewery, and more often than not sampled the wares. Father met her on the road one day and asked her if they would be having a Christmas, but she said no, that wasn't likely. It was always the custom to invite anyone in the community who might not otherwise have a festive Christmas, so Mother and Father invited the two young daughters of this woman to spend Christmas Eve with us.

We had eaten our lovely meal, we had danced

around the tree, we had sung our Christmas songs. Now it was time for Father to *hoste Jule-tre*, to take the goodies off the tree and distribute them among us. One by one he gave the sweets to each of us children. At last—oh, at last!—he came to the marzipan mask! He picked it off the tree.

"Oh, it's too bad we don't have one for each of you girls," he said, turning to the two visiting girls. "Instead you will have to divide this between you."

I thought I would faint. My marzipan mask! I turned and met Mother's eyes, and while I bit my tongue and said nothing, the look said, "That was mine!"

Mother only gave me a long look. "You will have to learn to share," she said.

On Christmas Day we had another big meal at noon and then we were supposed to rest. To a child that was the worst thing that could have happened. What a waste of time! Sometimes we would be allowed to use our skis a little. But Mother was intent on getting us to rest. She probably thought all the excitement of Christmas was too much for us!

God certainly had His real place in our lives, although Mother and I were the only ones who attended church regularly. We went every Sunday to *Tangen Kirke*, a beautiful all-brick church that sat on a little point high above the fjord. All around the church lay the *kirkegård*, or graveyard. Father rested at home and read the Sunday paper. But in those days the pastor's Sunday sermon was printed in the paper. So when we got home, Father would already have read it and I would have to report to him and he would make sure I had listened!

We had religious instruction in the schools, one hour each day. Then we went to special confirmation instruction for a year, about the time we were thirteen. It was a difficult time. I was growing and changing and not feeling well, and I had to make the long walk up some big hills to Skoger *kirke* for instruction each week. I would come home so very tired, and Mother would help me take my dress off. "Now go lie down, *jente min*," she would say.

The actual confirmation examination and ritual lasted three Sundays. Each Sunday we would sit in a row on benches that lined the center aisle. The pastor would quiz us on the catechism and Bible history and we would have to answer the questions one by one. On the third Sunday we answered more questions and then for the first time partook of communion. We girls wore black dresses, not white as in later years, and they were our first long dresses. Now we were grown up!

One of my friends wanted a dress exactly like mine for confirmation. She also wanted to spend the rest of that Sunday with me. Dressed in our long dresses, we went for a walk through the settlement. Young men lifted their hats to us. How exciting! But when we came within sight of home, where no one from the village could see us, we lifted our skirts high above our ankles and ran home like the children we were.

It was a time of many changes. Father was now at the ironworks, so we rented a place in town. Until the house was ready for us, we lived in a nice small apartment in a side building on the property. The name of the house was "Solitude."

This was a time when Oscar and I had a lot of fun. Our parents would go to bed, but we had other ideas of things to do. We had a phonograph and often we'd wind it up and dance in the living room. Sometimes we'd sing with the music, but we always warned each other, "Don't sing loud! Don't talk loud!" And sure enough, soon would come Father's voice from behind the closed door: "What are you doing up so late?"

The Drammen fjord.

And then, "Turn off the light and go to bed!"

Sometimes we went out, walking through the town. Daytimes we'd often walk to the woods. Oscar might take his rifle and do some target shooting.

Our house stood part way down a long hill that ended clear down by the ironworks. What a great hill for tobogganing! But it was also dangerous because of wagons coming through on a main cross street. Often a policeman would stand at this corner, arms outstretched, to stop us young people who insisted on sliding down the long hill.

How well I remember the day John and Oscar and I came shooting down the hill and saw the policeman at the crossing, arms outstretched. His name was Vegen. We shouted for him to get out of the way. Now, ordinarily the expression would have been, "*Ut av veien*," but because of his name we used another expression which also means "out of the way."

"*Ur Vegen!*" we shouted. But it was too late. We hit him fair and square and carried him along on the toboggan for a good stretch before he rolled off. When we stopped, we managed to scramble up to a big house near the ironworks, a house that held rooms for old people.

"Lotta," I gasped. "Lotta will take us in."

We dragged the toboggan into the house and up to old Lotta's room.

"Lotta, may we come in?"

"Yes, if it's Anna."

We stayed there until we were sure the coast was clear. And we took the long way home. From that day on, the policeman was known (at least to us) as *Ur Vegen!*

Old Lotta Andrine was, you might say, a little odd. She made and sold brooms to earn a little money. When she came to our house, Mother would buy a broom whether she needed one or not. Lotta walked barefoot most of the year, pigeon-toed, mud and dirt between her toes. A son Karl, called "Lotta's Karl," brought home a little money when he could.

Whenever we had butchered, Lotta Andrine was sure to pay us a call. Mother would lay out a clean, hemstitched linen cloth on the kitchen table (she used a good cloth even for tramps who came begging a bite to eat) and Lotta would sit down and eat. Soon she would cross her arms over her bosom and fall sound asleep.

"Shhh," Mother would warn us. "Lotta sleeps."

After a while Mother would say, "Do you want some more, Andrine?"

"No, thanks. Maybe I'll have a little before I leave."

Mother knew what she meant, and Lotta would have meat to take home with her. Blood *klub*, *sylte*, she got a taste of it all, especially when it was Christmas. More than anything else, my mother's treatment of Lotta taught me to respect elderly people and people who were "different."

My brothers' lives were changing, too, at this time. George got a job in Nøstebruk, a big sawmill, before he was sixteen. When he was only sixteen, he became foreman over eight older men. But as he grew a little older, he determined to go to school in Oslo and entered *Underoffisar Skola*. He studied there for four years and graduated first in his class; there was a big story about him in the paper. Then he enrolled in *Otto Treiders Handelskole*, a business college, and again graduated first in his class. He had a good job, but he developed "Amerika Fever," and as the saying went in those years of emigration, "no doctor could cure that." I think it was his curiosity and sense of adventure that sent him off.

John, however, was the first one to go to America. He had taken up shoemaking and was a first class shoemaker, but he was also determined to go to America. It was to Beloit, Wisconsin, that he went, and five years later George joined him there.

Later, when I also went, young brother Oscar declared, "I am the only one who has the sense to stay home." And he did stay in Norway.

Meanwhile, I had turned fifteen and wanted to earn some money of my own. So I got a job as nurse-maid to little Christian Engen, son of a Skoger couple at whose place Father had worked. Little Christian was then a year old. He had an older sister, Margrethe, who was then twelve. I was to have every other Sunday off but I got so homesick for my home and family they finally let me go home every Sunday. I loved little Christian and when I left on Sundays he missed me so they could hardly do a thing with him. At times they even let him go home with me.

Margrethe became my good friend, though I was a little older. I was to sleep with the cook, but she smelled so strongly of cooking odors that I got to sleep in Margrethe's room. In the evenings I would help her with her lessons or we would sit and embroider. She, of course, would go on to higher schools.

Much of the time was spent taking little Christian

for walks—*spasere*, we called it. Margrethe and I would go on long walks into the woods in summer and on skis in the winter. How we loved to be out in the snow!

By the time I was nineteen, John was writing to us about his adventures in America and urging me to come. He had a good job as a molder in an ironworks in Beloit, Wisconsin, and he thought it would be a fine city for me, too. But to leave my parents? How torn I was, pulled in two directions! But at last I settled on my course.

"Five years," I promised my parents faithfully. "In five years I will be back."

America Fever

Norway lost a greater percentage of her population to emigration than any other European country except Ireland. Although America had been taking Norwegians in before the Civil War, the end of the war and the passage of the Homestead Act provided a real impetus. In 1882, 29,000 Norwegians left Norway, and by the beginning of World War I, Norway had lost 676,741 residents to emigration.

Amagda and Hans Johansen, Anna's cousin and her husband, have written about the many who emigrated from Drammen, Anna's home town, around the turn of the century. For the most part they were young sawmill workers. In winter there was no work for them; any work that came available went to men with families, so there was nothing for young people. Ship tickets cost around two hundred *kroner*, so a fifty dollar loan from a relative in America covered passage and food.

Sometimes a Norwegian-American would come for a visit, and the young people became more eager than ever to emigrate. They devoured dog-eared copies of a most popular novel, *Husmannsgutten* by Hans A. Foss, a romantic account of how a young man could work his way up in the United States in just a few years. The hero, Ole Haugen, earns enough money to come back and buy the great manor house where his parents are caretakers—and he marries the manor house owner's daughter as well. What dreams that book inspired!

Most left in the spring in order to have the summer to seek work. In the winter the *amerikakofferten*, or America-chest, must be built, a small, simple wooden chest with handles for carrying and a good lock. In it must be a small compartment for letters, photos, keepsakes and perhaps a farewell poem from a special girl. The mother would pack an overcoat, one or two lighter coats and an Icelandic wool coat for winter. One wore dress clothes on the voyage—likely the same set the whole crossing. On top of all the clothes in the chest Mother laid the Bible and *psalm bok*.

They sang, "*Farvel du moder Norge*," whose last stanza promised:

> And should it ever happen
> As life goes moving on,
> That I return to old shores,
> Then will I here be drawn.
> For here my heart is homing,
> 'Twas here I had my start,
> And the mem'ry lives forever
> Through longing in my heart.

Other books, like *The True Account of America*, by Norway's Ole Rynning, raised emigrant dreams to a fever pitch. But letters from friends and relatives already in America probably inspired more of the exodus than anything else.

Even those who stayed behind were affected by these letters. For the writers spoke of a land where there was no class distinction, where there was no

powerful state church and one could believe as ı
wished, where every man (though no women as yet)
had a vote, where no one needed to struggle on a tiny
plot of rocky land. The letters helped bring about a
climate in which liberal reforms were enacted, including land reform to make larger farm plots available.

All of Scandinavia poured people into America.
In 1882, the year when 29,000 Norwegians emigrated,
64,607 Swedes and 11,000 Danes came to the United
States. Shipping lines from Gothenburg were inun-
dated with people wanting passage and boat trains
from Hull and Newcastle to Liverpool were filled with
Norwegians on part of the first leg of their journey.

Admittedly, Norway prospered to a degree from
capital which the emigrants sent to families back
home. In one year, 1912, the amount was estimated at
two million pounds. A few returned to their old
homes, bringing savings and often new skills.

But for the most part, those who had dreamed of
coming back with enough money to buy out the
town's richest landowner instead ended their days in
the United States and Canada, many struggling
through terrible hardships on uncleared land and
prairie homesteads. And some were never heard from
again.

*   *   *

I was on my way to America! It was September
20, 1907. I was twenty years old.

All I knew was that my brothers were there waiting for me and that I must earn enough to pay my passage back home again in five years. For I had given my
parents a solemn promise that I would stay no longer
than five years.

Much has been written about the hardships of
crossing the Atlantic to the new land, even in the days

of steamships. But I had a wonderful time on that voyage, which lasted fourteen days. A friend and I had a third class cabin, but the fall weather was still good enough that there was dancing on the decks and we made many friends. The only person I knew beforehand was a man named Hans Hansen, but I came to know many as my friends, especially a nice young man named Martin Bekke. Some of the passengers had brought accordions or violins or mandolins, so there was music—and dancing, too.

We met a woman who was traveling to America to meet her husband, who had gone on before. She had small children with her, including a newborn baby, but she could not afford a cabin, even on the third class level. She had two beds down in the hold of the ship, but there was terrible noise from the ship's engines and they could not sleep.

"Are you game?" I asked the friend who shared my cabin. "We'll let her take our cabin and we'll go down and sleep in the hold."

"Fine with me," came the reply. How happy that woman was! Two beds in our cabin felt like heaven to her. I can still see the lovely smile on her face when we asked her if she had slept well.

But there was heartache on the voyage, too. Another young woman was traveling with her two small daughters to meet her husband in America. He had gone ahead to make a home for them and was to meet them now in New York. How happy they were! But one day we didn't see them on deck, and someone said the children were ill. In two or three days the youngest girl died, of diptheria, it was said. There was a Lutheran minister on board and he conducted a funeral service; the ship's band played and we all sang hymns. The next day the second daughter died, and again there was a funeral on deck, and the little canvas-wrapped body was lifted over the side. That poor mother—she looked as if she might pass out at any moment. And when the ship docked in New York, there was the husband to meet her and she must tell him the sad news. What a shock!

Before I left home, my mother and my aunt had warned me strongly against going places alone or talking to strangers. (Somehow the young men from my own country didn't seem like strangers!) A woman on the ship who was traveling to Chicago also took me under her wing. Many young women, she explained, were lured into white slavery by being too trusting of strangers.

Not long after, I was standing at the rail of the ship when a handsome older man came over and struck up a conversation. He told me he had made this journey eleven times, and that he knew both America and Norway well. He told me he spoke several languages. After a while he said,

"There's no need for you to stay in third class—you can move up to first class. I have more suites than I need."

I told him, no, thanks, and moved off.

Later that same day, my bunk mate, who was only sixteen, came rushing into our cabin. Her face was flushed and she was all excited.

"I'm going to pack," she exclaimed. "I'm moving to first class. There's a man there who says he has more suites than he needs and I'm welcome to one of them."

"Oh, no, you're not!" I told her and proceeded to shove her suitcases back. Then I sat down and explained to her what she may have been ready to walk into.

On one of the last nights before we docked, I dreamed that I saw the Statue of Liberty rising up in front of me. I also dreamed that as we were coming into the harbor, I saw a man on a balcony beating a rug. The next day, there was the Statue of Liberty just as I had seen her in my dream. And when the ship moved nearer the dock and I gazed out at all the buildings, there on a balcony was a man beating a rug, exactly as I had seen him.

I also dreamed that a young man came to meet me wearing the shiniest shoes I had ever seen. And so he did—later.

We docked and went through the immigration formalities on Ellis Island. I remember an Italian boy, a nice young man who looked as if he was frightened to be alone. I wish now I had been nicer to him.

Small boats took us from the ship to Ellis Island. It is hard to describe the crowds, so many people! The young man said, "Please, don't let them part us." But men threw heavy ropes to separate us into groups, and I never saw him again.

The first stop was a quick physical exam. Some were turned away immediately and sent back, especially those who were mentally retarded or showed signs of serious illness. Others who had less serious medical problems were whisked off for further examination. The place was so big, so many buildings, so much confusion.

Then we all had to go past the Immigration Inspector. This is where many Norwegians and Swedes got their names changed. If the inspector couldn't pronounce the name, or couldn't spell it, he might set down a different spelling that was simpler. Some were given the name of the town or farm they came from. I was lucky. I got to keep my name.

There were two women on the ship who took me under their wing. They told me, "When we say yes, you say yes. When we say no, you say no!" It helped.

From New York I took a train to Wisconsin and finally reached Beloit. Once out on the depot platform, I stood and looked around frantically. There was no John in sight. Where was he? He had promised to meet me. Suddenly a man leaned over beside me and tried to grab one of my suitcases.

"No, no!" I shouted.

A blonde young man stepped up. "Are you Anna Guttormsen?"

"*Snakker du Norsk* (do you speak Norwegian)?" I asked quickly.

"A little. I am Alfred Fossum."

"Oh, Alfred," I cried, "how you have grown!" The Fossums had moved to America from Drammen some years earlier. Alfred's oldest sister Gudrun had been my friend at home.

John, it turned out, had had to work late so he had sent Alfred to tell me to wait until he could get there. And the man trying to grab my suitcase was a taxi driver. We didn't need him for we were taking a street car.

Before long John was there. Relieved and happy, I looked my brother up and down. He was wearing a gray suit and patent leather shoes, the shiniest shoes I had ever seen!

"Did you remember Alfred?" John asked, laughing. Then he put his arm around me. "You are the nicest looking immigrant I've seen yet."

John was boarding with a Mr. and Mrs. Halvorson. "But you're invited to our house for dinner," Alfred told us. I was so excited at seeing those old friends again and learning that Gudrun was to be married. I stayed with them until after the wedding, three weeks in all.

But I was anxious not to outstay my welcome. Also, I was eager to begin earning some money. And since I had promised to stay no longer than five years,

I was determined to learn as much as I possibly could in that time.

So Anna Marie from Norway went out and found herself a job doing housework for three dollars a week.

Mr. Wright and his sister, a woman of about seventy, lived in a large house and roomed and boarded six college professors from the nearby college, where Mr. Wright also taught. So with me there were nine in the "family."

Picture me trying to learn new ways and a new language, all the while doing work that would have kept three people busy. I washed a big washing on a washboard every Monday morning. On Tuesday everything had to be ironed and I was up at four a.m. in order to get it all done. The ironing was done with sad irons heated on a gasoline stove in the basement. I was terrified for fear the stove would explode. Long table-cloths and linen napkins had to be ironed wet. Sheets and pillow cases all had to be ironed. All the beds had to be made every day and all the dishes and pots and pans washed.

The lady was very cranky. One day in the kitchen she said, "Go down in the cellar and get the lard."

I guessed at "cellar" because it sounded like *kjaller* in Norwegian. But I had no idea what the word "lard" meant. So I brought up some wood.

"No, no," she shouted. "Bring up the lard!"

I went down again. I looked around. Then I brought up some coal. She must want a good hot fire.

This time she stomped her foot and went down herself and brought up the lard. She tried to hide it so I wouldn't see it, but I saw and I never forgot that word.

After a couple of months I had learned more of the language and was also learning to cook. One day I was to do the cooking all by myself and also wait on the table.

All went well. I had served the soup, the salad, the meat course, and had just brought in the apple pie. I had made it myself and was so proud of it. At that time, pie was not widely known in Norway, so I felt it a real accomplishment to learn to make it.

Then it came. "And the cheese," said the lady of the house.

Cheese? I had never heard the word. I went back into the kitchen and looked around. Maybe they wanted knives for the pie. So I brought in knives. I was barely back in the kitchen when the bell rang.

"Bring the cheese!"

She must mean they need more water, I thought. I brought water and filled the glasses, which were already almost full.

"The cheese – the cheese – the CHEESE!"

I went over to her with tears in my eyes. "I don't underforstand," I said.

She didn't answer. I went back into the kitchen. The bell rang and rang but I did not go in. Then she came, her skirts swishing, and took something from the pantry and swept into the dining room. The bell rang.

"NOW," she said, "pass the cheese."

There was the *ost* that had been standing in the glass door cupboard. I didn't know it was supposed to be served with the pie. I took the cheese and passed it to each person. When I came to the youngest man, a professor in languages, he said,

"What do you call cheese in Norway?"

"*Ost*," I replied, and broke down and cried. I set the cheese down and fled to the kitchen. Oh, if only I was back in Norway where they didn't treat people like this woman does!

The young professor came into the kitchen. He

thanked me for the good dinner.

"And that apple pie! Did you make it?"

"Yes," I answered, and cried some more.

"That was the best apple pie I ever tasted." He sat down beside me and wanted to visit with me, but at that moment the landlady came back in and he left. Even the boarders were afraid of her.

One day she had me drag the big living room rug outside and beat it with a rug-beater, first on one side and then on the other. A nice old gentleman came by and stopped to talk. I couldn't understand what he said so he repeated it very slowly:

"That's nigger work, my girl."

I stopped and thought. I had seen black people by that time, doing hard work that no one else wanted to do. "Work," I knew what that word meant.

I walked into the house and laid the rug beater down in front of the landlady, who sat rocking in a rocking chair.

"Me no nigger," I told her.

She was furious. She went out, rolled up the rug and came dragging it in. She was breathing hard and her face was fiery red. I was so afraid she was going to drop dead that I went and hid.

After three months there, I went out and got myself another job. But even then the woman tried to stop me from leaving. When I think of all the dishes I washed in that place, it scares me!

I enjoyed my next place, though I worked hard there, too. There were two little ones in diapers, lots of washing by hand, and lots of babysitting. After a while I was getting five dollars a week, considered a good wage. Then I worked at Len Miller's, with three in the family. I loved it there but worked hard as usual. They entertained a lot.

And then my five years were almost up and I had

saved enough for my passage home. John had planned
to go with me for a visit, too. But while he had made
good money, he had also spent it and didn't have
enough for passage. George, meanwhile, had had di-
fficulty getting a job in Beloit and had trouble learning the language. He wanted to go to Seattle—as he
eventually did—and tried to persuade me to go with
him. But John discouraged it, saying, "You know what
you have here; you don't know what you will run into
out there."

I could hardly wait to get back to Norway! The
ship docked in Oslo. I took a train to Drammen. The
train depot was a big one and out in front stood a row
of horses and carriages waiting to take passengers. I
picked the first one in line and was amazed to find the
driver was a man I knew.

"Well, if it isn't Anna Guttormsen!"

"Yes, and I want you to take me home."

I climbed into the carriage. But first he stopped at
the shop where my brother Oscar was working as a
watchmaker.

"No, but Anna, is it really you?" cried Oscar.

Then we went on up the familiar street to our
home. I walked into the house. Father was in the
midst of putting together a bedroom set he had
bought, planning to have it ready when I got home. I
grabbed him and cried, "Come on, Father, let's have a
dance!" And we went whirling about the floor.

Mother was at the store when a neighbor spied
her. "I see there is company at your house. And I think
I saw your son carrying in an *Amerika kista* (America
trunk)."

"*I Jesu nam!*" cried Mother. Setting her groceries
down, she went running home. When she flung open
the door, there were Father and I still dancing about
the room. There were tears in his eyes and I was

almost afraid he would faint. For a moment Mother just stood in the door and took it all in.

Happy as I was to be home, I had really only planned to stay three months and then return to America again. But Mother got sick and needed surgery and I stayed to care for her. She recovered, but begged me to stay in Norway. It was to be five years before I again boarded a ship bound for America, and then only because my parents knew that my brother John really needed me.

Those five years were spent in Oslo, and they were happy ones for me.

An Oslo Interlude

It would have been difficult for Anna to re-
main in Drammen after those five years in America.
Drammen was home, yes, but it was also a mill town,
its precarious economy largely dependent on the sawmills that were its main industry. While Anna's father
had a secure job in the ironworks, there were many
who did not. Women and children as well as the men
worked sporadically in the sawmills.

Anna's cousin Amagda Johansen and her husband Hans some years ago gave a moving account of
turn-of-the-century and pre-World War I Drammen
in a book, *Der Far og Mor har strevet* (*Where Father and
Mother Toiled*). Hans's mother was widowed early and
she worked in a sawmill along with most of her six
children under the age of fourteen. Hans was five and
a half when he started at the mill. One of Hans's
brothers sorted poles as they came down a chute from
the trimmer. Another moved them to the pole yard.
Another son stacked them while the mother and
Hans handed them to him. Work started at six in the
morning, and when the pole trimmer finally
screeched to a halt at 9 p.m., the family could not

leave until the last pole was stacked. School had to be somehow sandwiched in between time at the poley-ard.

Amagda recalls working in a *fabrikk*, a spinning mill, around 1910 at the age of fourteen. She was the oldest child and the family needed the income. The mill was an hour's walk away, often in drenching rain. She had no rain gear and no extra clothes to change into when she reached the mill, so there were many days when she worked the long shift soaking wet. "I stood ten hours a day at the machine. Then I walked home in the dark, afraid of ghosts and drunks — yes, and of the gypsies who came in the summer and stayed so late in the fall that the gypsy children were running around barefoot in the snow."

Many men fished and sold salmon for extra income. Since the law stated that boat owners got two-thirds of the catch and the helper a third, it was important to take family members out as helpers. Amagda remembered going out with her grandfather, fishing through the night until dawn paled the sky to the east. Hot coffee kept them awake; each boat owner brought a big iron pot with wood in it and made a fire during the night; here the coffee pot bubbled. Boats with small fires in them made spots of light all over Drammen fjord. "But we never ate the fish," said Amagda. "It had to be sold."

Hans recalls an old teacher in his elementary school who understood that food was not always plentiful in the homes of her pupils. When the pinch of unemployment was at its worst in winter, she would sometimes bring a basket of heel ends of bread loaves which she divided out to the children. "None of us youngsters knew where she got the crusts. Later, I've thought that they may have been from some cafe or a hotel, for they couldn't serve crusts to their guests."

Anna's family knew no such privation. But after the excitement and optimism of America for five years, Drammen with its limited opportunities held few challenges.

Oslo, on the other hand, was the capitol city. (It was still called Christiania at this time; not until 1924 did the Norwegian Storting vote to return to the city's old Norse name.) It was an expanding city with a promise of jobs, the chief trade port of Norway. The Storting, or Parliament, met here, and from that building and the city center a system of city parks led all the way up a long hill to the Royal Palace. Along the way lay the University, called Royal Frederick's University until 1939 when it became the University of Oslo. It held murals by the celebrated Edvard Munch and had installed its first woman professor in 1912. "Many times in summer," Anna recalled, "I took my lunch and my embroidery and went to sit on a bench in front of the University. I could hear the Royal band up the hill, playing its noon concert for the King. I worked on my Hardanger tablecloth, and many of the students crowded around to see what it was because they weren't familiar with it." .

Culturally, Oslo was a live, spirited center of the arts. The National Theater, completed in 1899, was a beautiful building nestled into the downtown park system. The coming of independence was still re-cent enough to provoke impassioned discussion on what Norway and its people should become, and home gatherings could turn into boisterous debate sessions. Henrik Ibsen, who died in 1906, had come back to spend his last years in his native land, and his plays and his words still stirred the Norwegians as they did much of the rest of the world. Imagine the discussions provoked by a quote like this from one of his speeches:

"An aristocratic element must come into our life . . . .I am of course not thinking of aristocracy of birth, emphatically not that of money, nor of the aris-tocracy of knowledge, not even of that of ability and talent. But I have in mind an aristocracy of character and mind and will. It is only that that can make us free."

But it was not only their own poets and playwrights that were hailed by Oslo citizens. Anna remembers going to see "The Merry Widow" three times with her friend Marta Hansen, who was for forty years head of the cleaning women in the Storting. "I can still sing some of those songs in Norwegian!"

Certainly there was a striking contrast between Drammen and Oslo at that time. But how much more dramatic must have been the contrast between Oslo and the Montana prairie, where only weathered shacks and leaning barbed-wire fences broke the stretch of waving grass as far as eye could see.

*   *   *

I was still trying to make up my mind whether to stay in Norway or return to America.

"I'm going in to Oslo," I told my parents at last, "and see if I can get a job in that big shoe store I like so well. If I can, I'll stay. If I can't, I'll go."

I was twenty-five and even after seeing New York, Oslo looked big and exciting. I sought out the cashier in *Gransen Skotoi Magasin*, a large shoe store, and asked to see the manager.

"He's up on the third floor. Would you like to go up or shall I have him come down?"

"Have him come down, please."

When he came, I asked, "Is there any chance of an opening?"

"For what?"

"Selling shoes."

"Do you speak English?"

"Yes, a little," I replied in English.

"You speak it better than I do. You have a job! When can you start?"

"I must tell you I've had no experience."

"You'll learn."

We sold Queen Quality American-made shoes for women, men, and children. I worked near the big front door where I could give information to customers coming in. There were quite a few foreigners coming in and out of Oslo at that time. One day a big Russian came in and explained by gestures that he needed shoelaces. He gave me a ruble tip for understanding him.

It was a fine time to be young in Oslo. Not only were there many of us young people who banded together and made our own fun, but there were many young women working in the shoe store and we developed a real closeness.

I had a special little mission in the store. If there was something I realized the girls didn't like, I would write a little poem about it and tack it on the third floor bulletin   board, and soon changes would be made.

For instance, there was a stove in the middle of the store. It would be red hot on cold mornings but it was inadequate for the space and the room was cold. I wrote a little poem about how nice it was to hug the little stove after walking a mile to work on a cold morning, but think how nice it would be to have a new stove. It wasn't long and a new stove was there! One of the women typed them; no one else knew who wrote them.

No one wanted to work during the noon hour, the hour when the working men were off and would come to the restaurants to eat. I offered to work that hour and so got credit for an extra hour. I took all my noon dinners at a steam kitchen. Here everything was steamed—fish, meat, everything, so all the flavors

Anna (third from left) and friends from the store enjoy a picnic.

were left in the food. Here, too, I could drink cultured milk with a little cream in it. The others wanted to eat in fancier places.

There was a whole block of steam baths not far from the store, and I went every Friday night. When you first came in, there was a woman who washed your feet, arms, and hands with a brush and soap. Then you went into a huge steam bath, men and women in separate parts of the building. From there you went into a sauna-like room, where you sat on chairs or lay on benches. The dead skin would just roll off your body, taking any dirt with it. You ended up with a cold shower and a rubdown. Then into the fresh night air and the long walk home to the place where I rented a room in the apartment of Fru Olsen and her unmarried daughter. Part of the way led past *Var Frelsers Gravlund* (Our Saviour's Graveyard). I still remember the address of the apartment: *Yllevoldsvagen sotton*. I lived on the fourth floor and there was no elevator.

Of all the young men and women working in the store, I was the only one who had been to America. They all wanted to learn English and asked if I would teach them.

"It'll cost you something," I told them. "I'm going to charge ten cents an hour."

They crowded into my little room and sat everywhere while I taught them. We'd have coffee, too. One of the girls, Anna Gabrielson, had a brother who had a *konditori* wagon and often he gave her samples of cookies and other goodies.

Anna Gabrielson went to America during one of those years I was in Oslo. On the ship going over, she was eating at a small table. At the next table sat four men. One volunteered that he was from England. Because Anna had learned a little English from me, she could converse a bit with him. He said, "My father is a baker in England." She said, "My father is a baker, too." She went to her grandmother's house in Chicago; he stayed in New York. They wrote to each other, and one day he showed up in Chicago and they were married.

In winter young people from all over the city took their skis and rode a street car to the mountainsides that were just outside the city. Here was a big lodge with a stone fireplace. We warmed ourselves here and sat around it, singing and telling stories.

The boys would buy torches to light the way. You could see skiers coming by the line of torches in the dark. We roamed over the hills, climbing over fallen trees and fences. When we came to a fallen tree we'd put our skis parallel to the trunk and lift one foot over, then the other. We skied downhill with the torches, too, and if anyone fell they would quickly stick the torch in the snow so it wouldn't hurt anyone, and so no one would run into them.

If it was early when we got back, we might go

Returning to the boat after a day in Bygdøyness.

to a restaurant for a bite to eat; if it was late we might just stop for some *smørbrød* (sandwiches) and a good cup of coffee.

Sometimes we would go to watch the ski tournaments at Holmekollen, and I would remember how John had skied in tournaments here while he was still at home. He had won a diamond ring, a diamond stickpin, and other beautiful things for being such a good skier. He had brought his beautiful skis with him to America.

In summer our most special entertainment was to take a small boat from Oslo to Bygdøyness, a lovely park that was a sort of entertainment park. Sometimes we'd bring a *smørbrød* with us; we could buy coffee and *brus* (a soft drink) there, and all we had to worry about was catching the last boat back to

Oslo.

A wonderful singer came every year from Sweden – how I wish I could remember his name! What a beautiful voice he had! And he opened every night with the same song in Swedish:

> *De var på Bygdöyness en sommar kväll,*
> *Jag fick en piga kär och det var dig.*
> *De käre minne jag bevarar har.*
> *De var på Bygdöyness, de var i Maj.*

> It was on Bygdoy isle one summer eve,
> I found a maiden fair and it was you.
> The sweetest memory I carry here
> (with his hand over his heart)
> It was on Bygdoy isle, it was in May.

The girls would all cry, "Was it me? Was it me?" And he would slowly look over the crowd, from one to the other of the girls. Ah, he had such a way with them! I remember that he married the daughter of a riding master.

The 17th of May, Norwegian Constitution Day, was a high holiday. But for us at the store it was just another day of work. An especially busy one, in fact, for many people came to town that day and many wanted to buy shoes.

I can remember a little of the turmoil that led up to Norway's independence from Sweden. (May 17 did not mark that day, it marked the day Norway got its own constitution and came out of rule by Denmark into limited rule by Sweden.) There was much talk of war. One young man in the community was called up for service. He had recently married and had to leave his young bride. Everyone was so worried. He came to see us; he was crying. "I don't think I will ever see you again." But he was only gone a couple of weeks and then it was all settled and Norway was a free and independent nation, and there had been no war.

During my childhood days, we celebrated May 17 by marching in a parade in Drammen, carrying a flag—and with a new summer dress, if possible. We celebrated Midsummer Day, too, though we did not dance around the maypole as is the Swedish custom. We decorated our houses inside and out with greenery—branches and flowers. It was to celebrate, not the month of May, but *maj*, the greening of the earth in summer. Sometimes we went on a boat called a *lorje* on Drammen fjord. The boat was trimmed with birch branches and there was music and singing aboard. We would go to a gathering place beside the water, and there was much singing of songs about home and the beauty of the land. Sometimes Mother would simply put up a lunch and we would go up into the woods and enjoy the long summer day.

And while we marked the day in Oslo, too, May 17 and Midsummer Day were both work days unless they fell on Sunday. We didn't mind. We simply enjoyed being part of all the activity in the city.

One day one of the women in the store said, "Let's go to a fortune teller tonight! I hear there is a good one down in Vika."

A fortune teller! A little shiver ran through me. Mother had always said they got their power from the devil. I wasn't sure I wanted to go. And yet I was as curious and as intrigued as the others.

When we came down the narrow, dark street, we spied some children playing in the street.

"Is the fortune teller's house nearby?"

They pointed to a house a few doors down. "Are you going to have your fortunes told? She's a good one!"

Uneasily, we approached the dark little house. A plank led up to the door; when you stepped on one end the other end went up. We could see a dim light coming from under the door. We rapped.

"Come in!" Then, "One at a time."

The first of the girls went in. When she came out she whispered, "Boy, she's awful looking!"

The second girl came out shaking her head. "She sure knows things. It must be the devil that tells her."

Then it was my turn.

She barely looked at me before she said, "You have crossed great water."

"Me?" I exclaimed innocently.

"Don't say that to me. I know. And in two weeks you are going back."

I smiled. Now she is talking through her hat, I told myself.

"You work in a store and you are handling black goods. In the place you work, there is a door in the corner of the building, but there is more than one door."

"You have seen me!"

"Never. When you come back to that store in the morning, there will be a letter waiting for you. That letter will change your life."

I don't remember if I slept that night, but I was fearful, waiting for the morning. When the store's mail came that morning, there was a letter for me from John.

"Anna," he wrote, "you must come at once, catch the first ship that leaves Oslo for New York!"

The story came out little by little in that letter. John had, like many newcomers of the time, been attracted by the news of free land in the West. He had left Beloit and had taken up a homestead near Malta, Montana, in a small settlement named Content. He had 320 acres of land on which he was "proving up."

Right next to him was another half section, 320 acres, not yet taken. If I hurried, I could take up homestead rights on that and if I lived on it part of each year and met certain other requirements for three years, the land was mine.

"We can farm it together," pleaded John. But there was still more to the story. In Beloit, John had met and married a fine girl named Loraine Gard. Together they were making their home on the new land. But Loraine was pregnant, and afraid of being alone with no other woman near.

At home with my parents, we pored over John's letter again. To all of us, the important thing was that John needed me. Loraine didn't like the open prairie, he wrote. It was too lonesome. There were few women, only men for neighbors. She couldn't get away to go anywhere. She was afraid to stay alone. John was afraid she would continue to be unhappy.

"We can't let this happen," said Mother at last. It was decided that I should go.

Back in Oslo, I went to one of my bosses. I said I had to leave for I was going to America.

"We don't want you to go," he told me. "You can set your own wages if you give up this idea."

"I like it here," I said, "and if I were going to work, I would work here."

"Are you getting married in America?"

"No, my brother needs me badly. He has taken up land."

"Well, Frøken Guttormsen, I have talked to our lawyer about these things and you have to give us three months notice."

"No, for remember what I said when I started work, that I would not recognize the three-months notice requirement."

In the end they told me I could leave anytime. But just to be sure I consulted a lawyer myself. He turned out to be the same one that handled the store's business.

"You are right," he told me, "for either in going to America or getting married, you need only give a week's notice. So go to the office, get your pay, and take off."

The next available ship going to New York was leaving from Stavanger. I traveled there to board it, along with Ibby, a girl from my own area who hoped to find work in America.

But my plans to reach John in Montana as soon as possible went awry. For when we arrived in New York, the city was in the midst of an infantile paralysis outbreak. The metropolitan area was under a virtual quarantine. No one was allowed to board a train leaving for the West.

Ibby and I were met by a friend of her father's, a man who had a hotel for immigrants who had no place to go. Sometimes people would come here looking for domestic help. One day a woman arrived to interview me and offered to hire me as a cook.

"Don't you want two?" I asked.

"No, I only have use for one."

"Then I will have to turn it down, for I have promised to stay with Ibby."

"Very well. To get you as cook, I will take her on as second maid."

It was a beautiful home in Wikatunk, New Jersey. There were just three elderly adults in the family — a single woman, a widowed sister, and an older unmarried brother. The family name was Herbert. We had heard that they were millionaires. We had quite some experiences there and I will say that's where I learned to be saving, to take care of every little thing.

For example, when baking bread we had a round wooden stick to stir the dough with. We had to wrap the end with a cloth so as not to scratch the pan.

When we finished we washed the cloth and put it away until the next time.

Ibby and I had a dining room to ourselves and had to wait to eat until the family had finished. But John, the young "flunky" who did odd jobs around the place, had to eat in the kitchen when we were done. His dinner usually consisted of fried salt pork, dry cottage cheese, and potatoes—every day. I had been given orders never to tell him what we had for dinner. But one day John asked and I didn't want to lie, so I told him we had had chicken. He got very angry and demanded that the older sister come to the kitchen at once. She did, and with some pretty bad language he told her to eat the same fare he did. I think he really scared her. His dinners improved after that and things went better.

Ibby, who was very musical, was delighted to find that John had an accordion, a *dragspill*. Now, *dragspill* can be literally translated "draw-player," a "draw-er" that makes music.

But John was shy about playing the accordion in front of anyone. He kept it on a high closet shelf. One evening, in the hallway, I heard Ibby call him (and Ibby's music was better than her English):

"Oh, John, won't you do something for me? Won't you take down your drawers?"

John came running out of the hall and almost knocked me over.

"John, why are you running?" I asked, trying not to laugh.

"That's no place for me in there!" said a red-faced John.

Ibby and I were given worn-out rags to use as dish cloths. They were so worn out that Ibby had to sew patches on them. I would keep asking for new dish cloths and I think the ladies finally got tired of finding them for me. One morning when we got up a new

Anna (right) and her friend, Ibby, on the boardwalk in Asbury Park, N.J. during their three-month stay in New York.

dish cloth was hanging there. And a strong one it was! A dish cloth made out of strong canvas to cover a horse's face, neck, and ears—bound around the eyes with leather! The ladies shouldn't have done that—it kept us in stitches all day! We put it on our heads, ran after each other, galloped like horses and laughed ourselves sick. When we were through that evening, we rinsed out the "dishcloth" and hung it by the ears on a line to dry.

The next morning a nice new cloth was hanging there.

One evening the two women came to me and, with a grin at each other, said, "You girls are so smart you must know how to play the piano?"

"Not I," I answered, "but Ibby is a wonderful musician. She was asked to play every day on the boat coming from Norway." They smiled and looked at each other. "Then you must come and play for us some evening." A few days later they asked us to dress up nicely (we dressed in our Norwegian costumes) and come in to the drawing room, and they asked Ibby to play.

"We don't play ourselves, but we 'understand' music," said one with a wink at her sister. Ibby hesitated a little and, as the old expression goes, they laughed when she sat down at the piano. But when she began to play, her audience listened with respect. From that time on we were their friends, and when we had to leave they even shed tears and begged us to stay. They took us to the "boardwalk" in New Jersey to a lovely dinner.

After three months I could finally leave New York. I wrote John to tell him what day I would arrive. But when I reached Beloit, my old friends there begged me to stop over and stay a week. Surely a week would make no difference. If John couldn't meet me after a week's delay, then I would simply take a taxi out to his place.

How little I knew!

The Homesteader

The original Homestead Act passed in 1862 offered farmers a free quarter section of land, 160 acres, provided they paid a small filing fee and lived on the land for five years.

But as time passed and settlers pushed west, it became clear that 160 acres could never support a family in the arid Great Plains and several further homesteading laws were passed. Finally, in 1909 came the law under which most of the Montana homesteaders secured their land. The Enlarged Homestead Act offered 320 acres—a half section. To land-hungry would-be farmers this seemed like a veritable bonanza. In 1912 Congress added the Three-Year Homestead Act, reducing the "proving up" period from five to three years. However, non-citizens still had a five-year waiting period, an impetus toward getting citizenship papers as quickly as possible. The 1912 law required the homesteader to live on his or her land only seven months of the year; he or she could spend the summer months away earning money to plow back into the land.

There was an explosion of promotional campaigns aimed at luring settlers. Jim Hill, the legendary kingpin of the Northern Pacific, Great Northern, and Burlington Northern Railroads, outdid all the hawkers, bankers, chambers of commerce and newspaper editors in touting the possibilities of these vast acreages. A flurry of leaflets blanketed America and Europe. The railroads offered low trans-Atlantic fares to immigrants and cheap rail tickets to all to their new homes. The railroads had cheap land to sell (in 1900, the Northern Pacific alone owned over 13 million acres in Montana) and were eager and waiting to move homesteaders and equipment and in time to ship the products they would hopefully raise.

With his eye on the latter, Hill threw his weight behind efforts to promote dry land farming, described as "agriculture without irrigation in regions of scanty precipitation." For it was becoming apparent that these regions, alternating between periods of adequate rainfall and years of cloudless skies and parched acres, could not be farmed the way the Midwest was farmed. For his efforts Hill had his defenders; others would agree with historian Joseph Kinsey Howard, who called him "nearly the sole architect of later disaster."

But the homesteaders came. Some, as Ed Hought and his brother had done, drove cattle over the plains from North Dakota. Most came by rail, often crammed into a boxcar between their cattle, machinery, household goods and food. Some came with not much more than a trunk. Many a Norwegian homesteader arrived with a barrelful of dry, unleavened Norwegian flatbread. They built rough one-room or two-room shacks, sometimes covered with tarpaper, other times simply lined inside with yellowed newspaper. If they could last out a few years, they added and improved.

Phillips County, where Malta and Content

are located, was once the eastern part of Choteau County and the western part of Valley County. Even after cattle were being run over most of the rest of the state, this region was still home to Indians, trappers, hunters and a few prospectors. Later came smaller cattle operations and sheep rangers. At the time Anna homesteaded, there were still vestiges of the sheepherders around, locations of old shacks, legends, stories — even, as John found on the prairie, their old cookstoves.

*   *   *

It was two a.m. on a September morning in 1916. The rain was pouring down when the Great Northern train pulled to a stop in Malta, Montana. The night was pitch black except for lights in the depot and a faint light or two from Main Street.

There was no one to meet me. Well, John would have had no way of knowing I was a week later than I had planned. I left my trunk in the depot and lugged a suitcase through the rain toward a lighted building. As I came closer I could see "Arcade Hotel" over a door. I pushed open the door and heard loud voices coming from inside. There was a pair of swinging doors and I pushed them open, only to find myself in a smoky saloon. It was full of cowboys, some leaning on a bar, some sitting at tables playing cards.

"I—I guess I got in the wrong door," I stammered.

"This is no place for a lady," said the man nearest me.

I went out quickly. The only other door opened to a dark stairway. I went up and into a large hall. There was no one in sight. I sat down on a bench and waited. Soon a man came up the stairs.

"Are you the proprietor?" I asked nervously. "Do you have a room?"

"No, I'm sorry. There's a big convention in town and all the rooms are taken." I wondered if the men I had seen downstairs were part of that convention! More likely it was cowboys in town celebrating after a long trail drive.

"I am a sister of John Guttormsen," I ventured.

"Guttormsen? Why, he was here a week ago to pick up his sister."

"Well, I'm the sister."

"I do have a room," he said at last, "only there's no furniture left in it."

"Is there a bed?"

"Well, yes, there's a bed, but that's all there is. There was a big row here last night and the place looks terrible."

"I'll take it. I'm tired. I've been sitting up on the train all the way from Wisconsin."

The room was all he had said—and more. Chairs and tables, splintered and in pieces, were piled up in one corner of the room. The door had been knocked loose from its hinges and wouldn't close tightly. I was scared. I didn't undress. And yet, after I covered the pillow with my scarf and lay down, I fell sound asleep.

It was about five in the morning when a knock sounded at the door.

"Who is it?" I was suddenly awake.

"The proprietor. Don't be startled. Everything's O.K. I have a ride for you."

I climbed out of bed. There was no time—or place—to wash. I tried to smooth down my hair.

Outside, the rain had stopped. It was cold. A short, fat man in a big sheepskin coat, cinched in the middle with a rope, was waiting for me. Even after he told me his name, John Haddy, and assured me he knew my brother "real well," I was uneasy. He wore his hat pulled down over black curly hair, and he had a big nose.

"So you want me to take you out to your brother's?"

"Yes, please, that would be fine. Where is your buggy?"

"Buggy? No buggy. That's my wagon over there."

I looked, and my heart sank. It was a hay rack. Furniture, boxes, sacks of feed and crates of groceries were piled high. In the front of the buggy was a high seat with no back, a seat so high that our feet hung down without touching the wagon rack.

I climbed up and John Haddy settled himself beside me. It was about six a.m. when we started the thirty-five mile ride. The road was not much more than a trail, and the rain of the last few days had formed deep ruts where wagons had gone through. These had frozen hard during the night. Time and again the wheels would drop into the ruts and the top-heavy wagon would lurch first one way and then the other. When it tossed one way, John Haddy in his big sheepskin would almost push me off the seat. When it lurched the other way, I would be thrown against him while I frantically tried to hang on to the seat.

On and on we went over what seemed like an endless desert. There was not a tree in sight. We never stopped, we ate nothing the whole way.

I thought about the community where John said his land lay. Content. What a name! How could anyone be content in this godforsaken place?

By about seven that evening, we had crossed what seemed to be the desert and saw our first hills. We started down one hill, somewhat off the trail.

"Where are you going?" I wanted to know.

"To somebody's house."

Sure enough, we pulled up in front of a dug-out in a sidehill with a little shed in front. Haddy jumped down, and numbly I climbed off the wagon. As Haddy began unloading grocery boxes, one per-

72

son after another came pouring out of the house.

"Come in, come in," they cried.

Inside was a single room with a stove and table but no beds to be seen. (They were raised up against the wall, with curtains between.) The family was in the middle of supper and they moved over to make room for us.

"Will you have something to eat?" they asked me.

"Oh, yes! Do you have any coffee?"

They told me later that I drank seven cups of coffee that evening. I was relieved to find that they had an outhouse down the hill a bit!

Living in the dugout were Mr. and Mrs. Lusby, Bob, Earl, Mary and Tillie. A son, Bill, and his wife Elida and two children were eating with them that evening, but they lived in a different place.

When John Haddy felt his horses had rested long enough, he was anxious to be on his way. We jolted on down the trail in the dark. Soon we arrived at another crude little house, not much bigger or better than the dugout shed.

Haddy pushed open the door and lit a smoky lamp. "Well, this is my place. You're going to have to stay here tonight."

I looked around. There was only one bed. As if he read my mind, he said, "You sleep there."

"Where are you going to sleep?"

"I'll sleep upstairs."

"There's no upstairs. Can't you make it to John's?"

"I could but the horses can't. I could barely get them this far." Haddy went to unhitch his team and put them in their shed. I sat looking around at what I was to find was a typical bachelor's cabin: a stove, a table, a bed, one chair and a smoky lamp.

After a long time, John Haddy came back in. "Well, I found my saddle horse. I'll take you home in the buggy."

I followed him into the night. "We're going down a steep slope here," he warned, "and it's dark so you hang onto me." We slipped and slid down the hill, not able to see a step ahead. Here was the buggy and soon John brought out a saddle horse and hitched it up.

Even with a broken spring jabbing me, it was a relief to be away from the hard, jolting hay wagon. I leaned back and tried to relax.

But suddenly I felt something around my neck, a feeling of something crawling over me. I sat bolt upright.

"What—what's that?"

"Oh, that. There's a mouse hole in the upholstery, see? They've sort of built a nest in there."

There was nothing to do but to take it. I rode with the mice. At least I knew what they were.

After a while we came to a neat looking high gate.

"Whose gate is this?"

"Your brother's," said Haddy as he climbed down to open it.

What a nice one, I thought. So like John, who liked things to look nice. "How much further now?"

"Half a mile."

At that moment there was an opening in the dark clouds covering the sky and the moon came out, big as a washtub. In the moonlight I could see a small house sitting down in the valley. How beautiful it looked.

We pulled to a stop in front of the house. Haddy didn't knock. Instead he threw a stone on the roof and it came rattling down.

John told us later that he dreamed someone had come to kill him. He jumped out of bed. "I have to see who is at the door at this hour!"

John and Loraine Guttormsen.

"John, don't!" Loraine cried.

"John," I shouted, "it's me, Anna!"

How happy and excited they were to see me! But I also got a good bawling out for not coming when I said I was going to! It turned out that on the day I had planned to arrive, John had walked the thirty-five miles from his homestead shack to town, carrying a horse blanket to keep me warm. He had planned for us to go back with the mail carrier. When I wasn't on the train, he hadn't dared leave Loraine alone any longer and caught a ride back to the homestead.

We talked and talked, and I think I must have slept around the clock that next day.

But brother John was in a hurry to show me the land on which he had filed for me.

And my shack.

"Shack" — how that word had puzzled us in Norway when John wrote about it. "There is even a shack on your land," he wrote. In Norway of course we pronounced it "*shock.*" What in the world was a shock, we wondered.

"Could it be a castle?" I had said to Father and Mother.

No, they didn't think so. After all, if a man had gone to the trouble of building a castle, he surely wouldn't be giving the land away. Still, I thought, wouldn't it be lovely if it were a castle, even a small one? Or was it a gold mine, perhaps?

The second morning John and I walked a quarter of a mile across a field. Here was a small, square shed of rough boards.

"Is this your chicken house, John?"

John began to laugh. "Anna, this is your shack, your house. See, you don't even have to build a shack on your own land, it is already here!"

My heart sank to my shoes. I barely heard John as he explained how he had filed on the land for me until I could get there to sign for it myself.

"It won't be so hard, Anna. We can farm it together. The law says we must live on our land five months of every year for three years. The other seven months we can go into Great Falls and get work so we have money to improve our land. At the end of three years I'll own 320 acres and you'll own 320 acres. And we can farm it together."

We opened the creaking door and looked in at the musty cabin. If there was one thing I had never wanted to be, I told myself, it was a farmer.

But I stuck it out. Three years.

John Guttormsen in front of Anna's prairie home.

At the end of that time I was thirty-two. I owned 320 acres of land. I had known three years of terribly hard work, work I never thought I would be able to do. I had known keen disappointments. One of the requirements of the law was that twenty acres be plowed and planted to crop. Beside the cost of the seed, planting itself was very expensive. We had no horses so we had to borrow them, and feed was very expensive. I planted wheat and thought, "I will get a bumper crop and have enough money to go to Norway!" But the first crop year was a dry one and I barely got back the cost of the seed. Each of those three years I went to Great Falls for the winter and did housework, and every cent went into improving the land.

I will never forget the fencing.

We fenced the whole 640 acres together. Since John had no horse, a neighbor who had been here longer and had a team and wagon brought the posts out to us. They cost ten cents a post plus the hauling. John and I dug the postholes in the unbroken prairie ground, he with a crowbar and pick axe, I with a post-hole digger.

After we had a row of posts in, it was time to string the wire. But we had no horse to haul the wire down the line. So I became the horse. John built a framework of two-by-fours that hung on my shoulders, with a board across my stomach and a two-by-four hanging down in back on which the heavy spool of barbed wire was hung.

I would bend over and pull the heavy load along. John would attach the wire to the posts. Then we would stop and dig more holes, put the posts in, tamp the earth down hard. Then I would push ahead with the wire spool. It would get caught in the sagebrush. I would pull and pull. My hips were almost raw and I grew so stooped from pulling that I couldn't straighten up at the end of the day. But somehow we were able to laugh even about that!

We ate very little, partly because we had little, partly because it was so hard to get certain things on the prairie. It was a mile and a half to a man who had a cow. The food we took out on the fence line might be a can of tomatoes with some dumplings in it. I grew so hungry for potatoes, but no one had any.

We worked for two half-year periods to fence our land. By the end of the second autumn, as I had the year before, I returned to Great Falls to get work for the winter. I found a position as a hired girl for a doctor's wife. Once when I bent over to pick up something, I exclaimed, "Ouch!" and the doctor's wife heard me.

"Anna, what is hurting you?" she asked.

I blurted out to her what I had been doing all summer.

"Well," she said firmly, "you are going to see the doctor."

I protested. I didn't want to. I was embarrassed and ashamed of the gouges from the two-by-fours that still showed on my body. But she insisted.

Anna and little Oscar in front of John and Loraine's home.

The doctor frowned. "What in the world have you been doing?"

"Fencing."

"Fencing? But how . . . "

"Well," I admitted, "I played horse."

I explained how we had been able to fence 640 acres in two summers without help and without a horse. The doctor shook his head. "You must never, NEVER do a thing like that again." And then he added, "Men and women are NOT built alike, you know."

Dr. and Mrs. Adams often had as guests a very famous couple—the cowboy artist and his wife, Mr. and Mrs. Charles M. Russell. I would have the honor of helping Mrs. Adams pick out an exciting menu. "The best would not be any too good for the Russells," she would say. They were both very quiet and polite. He would call later and say, "Thank you, Miss Anna, for the lovely dinner." I'll never forget him with a sterling silver steer's head on his hat and the same kind of ring on his finger.

But when spring came it was time to head back to the shack, to spring work, putting in the crop, improving the land. And yet, with all the work, with all the strangeness of the new country, with all the things we did without, I remember a feeling of being happy most of the time. I'm not sure why. I think much of it came from knowing I was being of help to my brother when he needed me.

Loraine had the baby in Great Falls. He was a beautiful boy and they named him Oscar for our brother in Norway. Loraine and I became good friends. Sometimes, even after a long day of fencing, I would walk the mile and a half to the nearest neighbor who had a cow to buy milk for the baby. Oscar was the light of our lives. How we loved that baby!

One of the first things I did was to fix up the shack (oh, I knew the meaning of that word now!) on my homestead. It was about twelve by fourteen feet in size. I think it had been built to store grain. It had plasterboard walls but no furniture. I managed to buy a cupboard from someone and painted it and put my dishes in it. John had found a cookstove out on the prairie, one that a sheepherder had left behind when he left the country. He dragged it home and hooked it up to my chimney. It leaked ashes, but do you know, I baked angel food cakes in that oven as if I thought I was somewhere else!

The cowboys who came around to see John loved to tell stories to frighten me.

"Anna, have you noticed that mound outside your shack?"

"Oh, yes, I've sat there many times."

"Well, there was a sheepherder killed outside your shack and he's buried there." Then they told stories of big ranch owners who would kill a sheepherder to take his pay back.

"What kind of a country is this anyway?"

"Well, Anna, Malta wanted to be in style and have a cemetery, so they killed an Indian to start one."

They had me so afraid of Indians and sheepherders that I told John I wanted a second door in my shack.

"What for?"

"So if an Indian or sheepherder should happen to come in, I could run out the other door."

"Don't you think he'd run after you?"

"He'd never catch me!"

One thing we forget in this day of big Montana farms, some of them a thousand acres, is that in those homesteading years there was usually a homesteader's shack of some kind on every half section. So we did have neighbors. Most of them were bachelor farmers, but they were usually willing to help out when needed.

Once, after John had acquired a horse and wagon, Loraine and I decided we wanted to go for a drive. John was off working in Great Falls as he did winters and whenever he could get away, in order to make some extra money. So it was up to us to hitch up the horse.

We worked and worked but nothing fit the way it was supposed to. We turned the straps this way and that, but could not make it fit. The longer it took the more we laughed; we laughed until we had to lie down on the ground, and the horse stood looking at us as if he wondered how two people could be so ignorant about his harness. At last, one of those bachelor farmers who had been watching us from across the field could stand it no longer. He came walking over.

"What are you ladies trying to do?"

"We want to go for a drive but we're having a terrible time."

"It might help," he said as he took the harness

out of our hands, "if you turned it around." We had been trying to put the front part in back and put up front the part that went under the tail. It must have been one of many good stories that farmer had to tell!

It was a great day when John got enough money together to buy a cow. Better yet, she was with calf. How we hoped it would be a heifer calf that would in time make a second cow for them. John had to go to work in Great Falls before the calf was born, but he made Loraine promise she would write him as soon as it happened and tell him whether it was a bull calf or a heifer.

One morning we found the cow had a beautiful little calf with her in the small corral.

"But what is it?" Loraine looked at me.

"I don't know. I don't know how you can tell. Don't you?"

"No, but we should be able to figure it out."

We looked and looked and felt and felt. But we couldn't make up our minds. All day we fussed over that calf. At last we thought we'd better put it in the pen John had built under the strawstack. I started to pull it in that direction but the calf braced its legs and would not move.

"Go on, have it your way," I muttered and began to push it. Finally I got it in the pen and shut the gate. The calf stood stock still.

Suddenly I shouted to Loraine, "It's a she!"

"How can you tell?"

"Look, look!" The calf was passing water.

Loraine looked at me blankly. "And what does that mean?"

But she went in and wrote to John, "The cow had her calf. Anna says it's a girl. Isn't she smart?"

One spring, a bachelor neighbor decided that Loraine and I should get started raising chickens. He brought over two setting hens, one for each of us, and a setting of twenty eggs apiece. We decided to keep them together in a little lean-to at Loraine's.

"Now, in twenty-one days," said the neighbor, "you'll each have quite a few chicks hatched out."

We counted the days. On the twenty-first morning Loraine appeared at my door. She looked stricken.

"Loraine, what is it?"

"Those eggs. It was twenty-one days today. And they hadn't hatched. So I . . . I . . . "

"You what?"

"I thought they were spoiled. So I took and threw them into that coulee behind the barn. And . . . and . . . "

"And what?"

"And the chicks are lying down there going like this!" And Loraine's fingers fluttered in front of her face.

There was no way we could get down that steep bank without risking our necks. We would have to find another way to get chickens.

I had given away my favorite outfit before I left Oslo – a two-piece brown suit with a velvet collar and a big hat with a real plume. I wanted new clothes to wear to America. I brought with me another nice two-piece outfit, green, and a beige straw hat with two long feathers up the side. I also had a gray pin-striped suit; years later I used it to line my husband's leather jacket.

There were so few opportunities to dress up. The church was so far away we never attended. Sometimes a man would come out from Malta to hold a service in the schoolhouse and we would go about fifteen miles to hear him.

There was one Sunday when I just decided to get dressed up even if I wasn't going anywhere. I put

on the dark blue silk georgette dress I had brought
with me from Oslo. But then I realized I needed something to burn in the kitchen stove. Since firewood was
so very scarce on the prairie, we were always gathering
up cow chips to bring home and burn. So I ran out on
the prairie in my blue georgette and started picking up
cow chips. Suddenly I looked up and realized a man
was walking by on the wagon trail. Later he told me, "I
saw you out gathering kindling," and I was so embarrassed. All I could think of was how ridiculous I must
have looked out there in my lovely blue georgette!

Incidentally, don't think that my homesteading experience was unique. At that time there were
many single women homesteading in Montana, many
of them young widows. There were actually a lot of us
out there burning sagebrush and cow chips for quick
heat.

As hard as we all worked, there were pleasant
days, breaks in the work load. I found that another
single woman was homesteading only two miles away.
She, too, had a little shack much like mine, and we
became fast friends. Her name was Emma Hought, a
name I was to come to know well before long.

Once Emma and I baked a cake together for a
party. Among other things it called for molasses and
soda. We forgot the soda. You can guess how flat and
hard it was! But, as in everything else, we tried to
make the best of it. We crumbled the cake up fine,
mixed in some water and soda and baked it again. It
turned out fine—we got a lot of compliments on it.

In a shack up in the Larb Hills lived a nice
looking young woman whom the cowboys in the area
had named "Sweet Marie." She rode a horse as well as
any cowboy. I remember her shack, for once a group
of us, including my friend Mary and myself, had gone
with a married couple on a trip of several days up into
the Larb Hills. It was the only place where firewood

Emma Hought, another single woman homesteader.

was to be found anywhere close to Content. But the ride, by horseback and with wagons, took several days each way.

Luckily, abandoned shacks could be found here and there along the route. Some were truly abandoned, others might be empty for a time while the owner was off working a cattle drive or on some distant ranch. In one we discovered an old bed piled high with straw; Mary and I eyed it as a comfortable place to spread out our bedroll and sleep. But the cowboys riding in the party warned us gravely that it was just the kind of strawpile that attracted rattle-snakes. Well! In another part of the shack was a table; it would be hard as a rock to sleep on, but at least we'd be off the floor. We had no sooner spread out our bed-rolls on it than the cowboys took over the nice soft straw bed in the next room!

We found Sweet Marie's shack empty, too, just in time for a night's stay. There was even a nice, clean quilt in a corner, which the cowboys promptly appropriated. But they had no sooner turned in than we heard, "Ouch! Ouch!" It seemed Sweet Marie had stuck pins throughout the blanket, probably to dis-courage wayfarers from making use of it as the cow-boys were doing. We relieved them of the blanket, I took the pins out, and Mary and I slept snugly that night.

The winters in Great Falls were a change, even though work went on in a different sort of way. I learned many things about cooking, baking and car-ing for a house. I learned different things from different employers. One winter I worked for Mr. and Mrs. Fisher of the Fisher Flour Mills family. She and I got along well; sometimes I had the feeling we were good friends, not maid and mistress.

And always I thought I would go back to Nor-way. I would have one good, big crop. I would have money for passage and more, and I would let John have my land, and I would sail home. But this was not to be.

Remember the dugout shack where we stopped that first evening and I drank seven cups of coffee? The two daughters there, Mary and Tillie, be-came good friends of mine. Mary would go in to Great Falls in the winters, too, so we saw each other there. And Tillie sometimes came to stay with me on the homestead.

Ed Hought.

In the spring of 1917, John and Loraine were still in Great Falls. Oscar had been born that winter, and John was working as a molder at the smelter. Tillie came to stay with me that spring. Since John and Loraine's shack was empty, she slept there but she spent the days with me and we took care of the two places.

The snow seemed to be melting all at once that year and the water was running through all the coulees. I'm not sure we could have got out of there had we wanted to. One morning Tillie had come over, but I was not quite dressed when someone knocked at the door. I was frantically trying to pull on my stockings while Tillie went to the door. When I joined her, I

Anna Guttormsen.

saw a nice looking man standing holding the reins of
an odd looking saddle horse. Behind him was another
rider, also on a strange horse.

"It's Ed Hought, " Tillie told me. "He wants to
know if we've seen any stray cows. His milk cows got
loose and wandered off."

"No, I'm sorry, we haven't seen any." Then,
wanting to make conversation, I said, "Nice saddle
horses you have."

Tillie giggled. "They're MULES," she whispered. I had never seen a mule before.

"Well," I shrugged, "they're still nice looking."

"They do have rather long ears," observed Ed

with a smile. He thanked us and the two rode off. But Ed came back several times that spring. Sometimes we went out together, sometimes we just sat and talked.

But young, unmarried homesteaders were not exempt from the call to service that was taking so many young men that year. The United States was completely involved in World War I. By summer Ed Hought had been drafted into the Army, and after a minimum training period he was shipped to France. There he was severely wounded in front line fighting—a piece of shrapnel went into his rib cage and came out through his back. He spent three months in a hospital in France, and for a time he was given up as almost dead. At one point a Red Cross nurse likely saved his life. Seeing the condition his wound was in, she found a doctor and insisted, "He must be operated on at once if he's going to live!" The wound was so close to turning gangrenous. He began to improve and was finally well enough to be sent to a military hospital in Utah. For a long time he got seven dollars a month as pension; a long time later it was raised to twenty-five dollars and over the years it was increased a little.

"Remember," the doctors told him, "you're only half a man now, so learn to work accordingly." But he worked like a man and a half!

The whole community at Content was happy to see Ed come home again. The first time he came over to our place his sister Emma and a neighbor man were with him. He was so pale, but his strength was returning. The neighbors organized a "Welcome Home" dance for the boys and Ed invited me to go with him. What an occasion that was! He was a handsome soldier boy indeed, and he proudly wore his uniform to the dance.

But winter was coming and it was time to go to Great Falls for work again. That winter we sent many letters back and forth between Great Falls and Content. In February, Ed made a trip to Great Falls to see me, and when he had been back on his farm a few days there came a letter from him asking me to marry him.

I wrote back and accepted his proposal, and on February 28, 1920, Edward Lawrence Hought and I were married in Great Falls.

Marriage and the Prairie

Anna's daughter Nora, who now lives with her husband Marlin on a ranch of their own, remembers the good times and the bad—and the funny. Of her early life, she writes:

"I remember when Mother ordered some pretty floral flannel to make my winter nightie. We talked and planned for it, and waited for the package to come. You can imagine our disappointment when we received black and peach-colored striped flannel, the stripes about an inch wide and running crosswise on the material. I looked like a little escaped jailbird!

"But it kept me warm. I slept upstairs until it became just too cold in the winter. By then snow was drifting in on the tarp that covered my bedding. I would undress downstairs, warm up next to the heater and make a mad dash upstairs. Mother, with a sweater on, would light the lamp and put a hot water bottle by my feet. She would help me say my prayers, blow out the light, and she was gone. I wiggled the water bottle around to warm up the cold spots,

listened to the elements battering the faithful house
and soon was asleep. When it grew so cold that it
would actually wake me in the night, my folks would
move the cot down to the kitchen behind the table.
There was little room for it, so as soon as possible I
was back upstairs.

"The best time of all to sleep upstairs was at
the time of the first spring thaw. The window would
be open, and I would hear the water roaring down the
coulee. What a marvelous sound to a drylander. Then
the smell of the earth awakening, and the sound of
birds singing their hearts out at dawn, and bright sunshine streaming in after the dark winter. Spring certainly was a release.

"But nature's best moments were not always
enough. The drought of the late 1920s and early
1930s took a great deal out of the spirit of the people.
Many of the homesteaders had already left for jobs
and easier living. Those who were still there couldn't
leave—they had no money, nor was their stock and
property worth anything. So it was to stay and struggle and wait it out as best they could.

"Mother worked hard in her garden. The soil
was as hard as baked adobe. No moisture, no encour-
agement. What little did grow was received with joy
and thanksgiving, for the garden was so important for
our food.

"The constant wind, the dust, the gloomy,
smoke-filled skies from fires in the Little Rockies, the
intense heat of summer, grasshoppers eating everything in sight, including clothes on the clothesline,
tumble weeds and drifting dirt piling up over the
fences, dams drying up, cattle looking for water,
hopes of a crop dashed each year—and all this at the
same time as the Great Depression.

"Bless their hearts, my folks didn't complain.
My dad would whistle a little. Mother sang a brave
song, maybe in Norwegian, or 'Red Wing' or 'In The

Gloaming' as she washed dishes or ironed clothes. They were always hopeful and trusted that things would go allright. Although they didn't talk about it a lot, I know they put their trust in God. I always felt secure."

Anna and her family were not alone in hardship. For a state that has some of the country's greatest water resources (both the Missouri and the Columbia Rivers rise in Montana), there is a real problem in distribution of moisture. And during Anna's years in the state, Mother Nature played some of her most disastrous tricks on Montana.

Until 1916, Montana had enjoyed a period of fairly ample rainfall. The state's average wheat yield was twenty-four bushels to the acre. In 1917, northern areas like Phillips County had a year of little rain; by 1918, the rest of the state was dried out, the beginning of a twenty-year cycle.

June of 1919 was the driest month ever recorded in Montana, and that year the average wheat yield dropped to 2.4 bushels per acre. Farmers were lucky to realize five dollars an acre from their harvest. Hundreds walked away from their homesteads that year, poor and beaten to the point that the Salvation Army came in to help when the government had nothing to offer. When word of the calamities trickled back East, land promoters hurriedly explained that these people were not cut out to be farmers in the first place. This canard put a burden of sorts on those remaining; they stayed out of pride.

The next year brought spring rain, then nothing more. The first dust storms clouded the skies that summer. With the great post-war need in Europe abating, wheat prices dropped sharply. By 1921, some regions were hit by wheat-stem maggots, others by grasshoppers and Mormon crickets.

The year 1924 brought rain and good crops in most areas. But for many it came too late. In the four years between 1921 and 1925, one out of every two Montana farmers lost his farm by mortgage foreclosure. Six years later in Hill County, which lies west of Phillips and Blaine Counties, ninety percent of all farm mortgages had been foreclosed. Between 1920 and 1926, more than half of the state's commercial banks failed.

Another cycle of low rainfall began in 1929 and lasted approximately ten years. In 1931, four-fifths of Garfield County, just south of Phillips County, needed help from the Red Cross to survive through the winter. The first good crop in four years came in 1932, but by this time the nationwide depression had forced wheat prices down as low as twenty-five cents a bushel – and it was often hard to find buyers at that. In 1933, 3500 of Daniels County's 5000 people needed relief help; this was the county that in the good year of 1924 shipped 2,750,000 bushels of wheat from Scobey! By 1935, a quarter of all Montana's population was on relief.

The Roosevelt administration and FDR's New Deal programs poured $381,582,693 into the stricken state from 1932 to 1939. Among the programs was a drought-purchase program to keep cattle from dying of starvation; 350,000 cattle were sold under this last-ditch measure. By 1939, war-time prosperity and a cycle of wet years brought better times to the northern plains. Agricultural planning, strip-farming, improved wheat varieties and larger acreages provide a better balance with nature. But even today there is an uneasy recollection of studies made on tree rings that indicate there have been drought periods here lasting as long as fifty years.

None of this scenario could have been imagined by an optimistic Ed Hought when he proposed by mail. Nor could Anna have imagined it as she started housekeeping and set about "making things nice."

*   *   *

Although there was no church near us in Content and we had seldom been able to attend services, we still considered ourselves strongly Lutheran. But at the time we wanted to be married, the pastor of the Lutheran Church in Great Falls was out of town. So we were married by the Methodist minister, in the parsonage parlor.

My wedding dress was made of blue georgette crepe with an underskirt, and decorated with white rosettes of beads on the skirt and on the bodice. John and Loraine "stood up" for us, also Helen Martinez and a buddy of Ed's from the war, Mr. Johnson. And all through the ceremony little Oscar, who was two and a half, sat on the piano bench and plinked on the piano keys with one finger. The minister and I looked at each other and nodded, agreeing that it was quite allright to have music during the ceremony.

Neither Ed nor I had much money. I had used all of mine on the farm and Ed had been away from his farm and unable to save much.

"Do you want a diamond ring or a trip to Minnesota?" Ed had asked me earlier.

"I'll take the trip."

"That was nice of you." I knew he was anxious to see his parents again after being away so long. And maybe he wanted to show off his bride, too!

There was time for dinner at a restaurant before we caught the train headed east. I'm sure I was too excited to eat much. Great Falls was having one of those wonderful weeks that sometimes come in February. A warm chinook wind had been blowing for several days and the snow was melting and the air was like spring. People were out in the streets in their shirt sleeves. When we got on the train, little Oscar waved and waved.

Anna on her Minnesota honeymoon.

But by the time we reached Minnesota, we were in the midst of a terrible blizzard. The snow was deep and getting deeper. Finally, in Bemidji, the train ground to a halt.

"Hurry," said Ed, "let's go to the hotel before everyone else decides to go there. This train will never get out of here tonight." Later we heard that the people who decided to stay on the train froze terribly.

When we reached the little town of Menagha, the snow was deep and the terrible cold continued. Ed's brother, Elmer, met us with horses and sled. Eight miles through the beautiful pine trees and we arrived at the Hought farm and a warm welcome. Theirs was a large and loving Christian family. Several of the twelve children were still at home. In those days, there was little indoor plumbing, even in town, and the outhouse must have been one of the coldest places on earth. I caught a bad cold.

I found that I enjoyed Ed's parents and his family. Ed and his sister Emma were the only ones who had gone West and the only ones I had ever known. The young people in the neighborhood had a big party for us.

On our way home we visited Ed's brother Jim and his wife Sophie in Noonan, North Dakota. The snow was so deep it completely covered a buggy in the yard. Jim had a coal mine, and our bachelor neighbor, Gust Peterson, was working in the mine. I went into the mine, came up behind him and surprised him.

"No, is it you, Anna?" he cried. "How did you get here?" I'm afraid I frightened him; he looked as if he had seen a ghost in the black mine. Ed and Jim stood behind us having their fun. Soon I was given a trolley ride to a place to get out of the mine.

We also visited Mamie and Ed Evenson and their nice big family. Ed had something to brag about—that Mamie had never seen him angry. When he felt like bawling someone out, he explained, he would put on his cap, go out to the barn, take off his cap, put it on the floor and tramp on it and talk to himself. No wonder Mamie is still living at past ninety-nine years.

When we returned to Malta and Content from our trip, we set up housekeeping on Ed's homestead in a one-room house with a small upstairs.

After the snow that had plagued the train in Minnesota and North Dakota, it was exciting to come back to the prairie and find that people were already in the fields. The chinook had not only melted the snow but had begun drying the earth and some were already plowing.

We were anxious to get into our fields, too. But there was one more thing to get out of the way.

"I just thought I'd tell you," said one of the

neighborhood bachelors when he stopped by one day, "that the fellows are planning a little shivaree Saturday night."

Yes, I had heard of those "shivarees" for newlyweds so I had a little idea what to expect. We blew out the lamp early that evening and went up to bed, but we didn't undress. For a long time everything was quiet. Then we heard them coming up into the yard. I expected to hear them banging pots and pans.

Instead, there was an explosion right underneath our window, and gunshots began going off, whizzing right by the window. I was terrified. I huddled in bed, too scared even to sit up. Outside I could hear people running back and forth.

At last we went down and opened the door to the "shivariers." Now, it was the custom in some places for the bridegroom to give the noisemakers a gift of money and with this they would buy drinks and food and stage a party a week or so later. But money was hard to come by on the prairie, and so they had turned the custom around. The "shivariers" brought a gift to the newlyweds.

But not money. When we opened the door, neighbors from all around crowded into the little house. Almost every couple, and every bachelor, too, it seemed, carried a burlap bag with something in it. Suddenly they all opened their bags—and chickens flew all over the house! They were wild! They flew on tops of chairs, they even flew up the stairs.

"Ed, Ed," I shouted. "They're going to lay eggs all over the house!"

The women had all brought food and the party began. But this wasn't all. Next Saturday night, I was informed, they would all be back for the traditional bride and groom's "feed," something the bride was expected to put on.

So all that week I baked pies—apple, mince, lemon and pumpkin. Luckily, I had brought the "makings" along with other supplies from town. They were all invited back — and they all came. (And maybe some more!) There weren't enough chairs, so they brought in chunks of wood to sit on. Some sat on the steps, all the way upstairs. When it was over, we felt that Mr. and Mrs. Ed Hought had been properly welcomed by the Content community.

That first spring of our marriage, our greatest concern was, of course, to get the crop in. There was Ed's land and the twenty acres that were cultivated on my land. But like many years we were to experience, the year turned out to be dry and there wasn't much of a crop. Again, my dream of a trip to Norway from the crop on my twenty cultivated acres faded.

But we were determined to make a home here. Ed broke ground for a garden. He had a small barn with a couple of cows and a team of mules. The "shivaree chickens" were housed in the barn with the cows.

There's a remarkable story about how we got the first cow after our marriage. When we visited Jim Hought on our honeymoon, he told us that one of his cows was lost on a cattle drive to summer pasture in Montana. He described her as a black and white cow with her ears and part of her tail frozen off, or "bobbed." She had dislocated her hip on the drive and had to be left behind. He told me that if anyone could find her for me, she would be mine, a wedding present from him.

When we got home, I began to describe her to the cowboys around there and asked them to look for her. After a while, one of the Armstrongs brought her in for me! She made herself right at home and after a while she freshened. I named her Nellie. She was a Holstein and a remarkable producer. Because of her, we had such good cheese and cottage cheese, milk and cream to use and butter to sell.

When Nellie got too old to keep, we had to send

her to the roundup. Ed and I stood at the window, watching with tears in our eyes as she was herded down to the Nelsons' to join their cattle and then those of neighbors on their way to the railhead.

As soon as we were back from Minnesota, I set about fixing up the house to make it homey. In time we laid new blue linoleum on the floor and installed a beautiful gray enameled Kalamazoo kitchen range. Believe it or not, I made curtains from cheesecloth – ten cents a yard – and they were pretty, filmy and soft at the windows. Apple boxes made extra cupboards with bright cretonne curtains hung in front. At first, the house had no double walls and the lumber that had gone into it had a good many knotholes through which the wind blew. We had no storm windows, although as the years went by we improved the house until it was warm and cozy even in winter blizzards.

But fuel for heating and cooking was always hard to come by. As I have said, there was not a tree in sight on the prairie. So Ed would take a team and wagon and go about forty miles to the Larb Hills, where the farmers could get wood.

On one of those days that he and friends had gone for a load and I was expecting him home, I had gone around with an uneasy feeling all day. When it was late in the day and he still had not come home, I had such a strong feeling that something had happened to him. Then I saw the team and wagon coming across the prairie. But someone else was driving. The man did not stop at the house but went directly to the barn and put the team in. I went running out to see what had happened.

"Ed's team got scared of something and took off," the neighbor explained. "Ed stayed on the wagon until they got right up to a cut bank and it looked like the team was going to go over. Well, Ed jumped then, but one horse fell, stopping the team just as they were about to go over the brink, so they're o.k."

But Ed had broken his knee. He had managed, with the help of his friends, to set it himself, but other neighbors had taken him by truck to the doctor, thirty-five miles further.

That thirty-five mile trip to town always meant that we had to plan very carefully for what we needed. No forgetting something and running to the store the next day! At first we only made the trip to Malta twice a year. But as time went by, we had grain to haul to the elevator. Then as our cows and chickens began to produce more than we could eat, we made trips to town to sell my butter and eggs. Well, not exactly "sell"—we exchanged them for groceries. I churned butter from sweet cream, keeping the cream down in the cold well. I had a cold dry well to keep the butter and eggs in. I always got a premium price for my butter—in fact, I would have to say I was known in the stores in Malta for having the best butter.

I never had good luck ordering from mail order catalogs, so whatever buying of clothes we did was done in Malta. It wasn't much, for I sewed almost everything. I made dresses and aprons from flour sacks even before I had a sewing machine.

But soon after we were married, I got my first sewing machine. And what a machine it was!

Ed and I were in Malta. As we walked by a second-hand store, I said, "Let's go in and see if they have any sewing machines." In Norway I had sewn on a Singer machine that had a handle on the wheel. You put the cloth under the pressure foot and needle, guided it with your left hand and turned the wheel with your right hand.

"A sewing machine?" The store proprietor chuckled. "Say, I've got one here you ought to see. You can't sew on it, of course, but you'll get a kick out of it."

He set it on the counter. It was a machine with a

handle on the wheel, almost like the one I had used in Norway, except that this was a White.

"Here," he said, still laughing. "I'll show you how it works." He demonstrated on a piece of cloth, but wouldn't have needed to. I knew how it worked.

"I'll take it," I said.

He looked surprised. "You can have it for nothing."

"No, no. We will pay you."

"Well, shall we say five dollars, then?"

He carried the machine out, still chuckling.

It was many years before I got another sewing machine. On this hand-propelled machine I sewed all my own dresses and all of Ed's work shirts. He was tall and had long arms and couldn't get sleeves long enough. When the collars got worn, I turned them. When the turned collars wore out, the sleeves and front were usually worn out, too. But the back was still good, so out of this I sewed aprons, even to the point of putting ruffles around them. I would iron them so they always looked nice. Some of the neighbor women would say, "How can you afford so many aprons?"

But there was another reason why I needed a sewing machine at this time in 1920. I was pregnant, and knew I would be sewing baby clothes soon. The thought of doing all that sewing by hand on top of all the work that regularly had to be done was more than I thought I could handle.

How does one plan for the birth of a baby in a home thirty-five miles from the nearest town? In our case, we decided to take no chances, and plans were made for me to go to Mrs. Ebaugh's Maternity Home in Malta to have my baby. I would go in early and stay at a hotel until the time of delivery was imminent. By that time, one of our bachelor neighbors had a car (yes, they were beginning to be more common but we didn't have one yet) and he took me in to Malta.

Nora Hought. Anna made her dress of white nainsook. "I used a thimble to mark the scallops around the bottom, satin-stitched them just as I had my mother's doily years before."

This was soon after the middle of November. We expected the baby late that month, and Ed made plans to come to Malta so that we could have Thanksgiving dinner together at a restaurant there.

The day before Thanksgiving Ed came to town. He was still in his work clothes and in his suitcase were the dress clothes he planned to wear. But when he reached the hotel and gave his name, the clerk said,

"Oh, Mr. Hought, didn't you know? Your wife had a baby girl three days ago."

"A baby!" Ed set his suitcase down and dashed out the door, heading for the maternity home.

Meanwhile, I had been waiting and waiting for him. I could hear people come up the walk and think,

"No, that man doesn't walk like him." Finally I heard a man coming up the walk and I recognized Ed's gait. "Oh, here he comes!" I cried.

"Mrs. Hought, how can you tell?"

"Oh, I can tell," I said. So the nurse met him at the door.

"Are you Mr. Hought?"

"Yes, yes. Where is my wife?"

"Come here. I have something to show you."

I can still see Ed as he took the baby from the nurse's arms and held her and stroked her face. "Oh, she looks exactly like me!" he said over and over.

At that point, on the third day, I felt well enough that I could have gotten up. But in those days mothers were supposed to stay in bed for two weeks after childbirth. By the time two weeks had gone by, I was really sick and weak and could in no way have gone home without help. The same neighbor came and got me but this time Ed's sister Emma came along to help with the baby.

By now it was shortly before Christmas and it was cold. There were no heaters in those early cars. They had made a bed for me in the back seat; Emma rode up in front with the baby in her arms.

"Are you warm enough, Anna?" she would ask.

"Yes," I'd answer from under the wool and horse-hide robes. "Is the baby warm?"

"She's just fine," Emma would say. "She's sucking on the thumb of my leather glove."

Let me pause here and tell you about Emma. She homesteaded next to Ed's homestead and her shack was near his. She and I had become fast friends and had many good times together. When she decided to quit farming, she asked me, "Maybe I should go find a job somewhere. Should I go east or west?"

"What do you feel like doing?"

"I feel like going east. It's as if something were

pulling me east."

Emma took the train, intending to go to her parents' home in Minnesota. Along the way she decided to stop and visit a relative in Starbuck, Minnesota, who owned a bakery.

"Do you need any help?" Emma asked him.

"Yes, I certainly do," he replied. "You can be our new counter girl."

There she met one of the bakers, a young man from Norway, Ole Berg. It was love at first sight. Soon they were married. Later they started their own bakery and raised a family. So what was that "something" that drew Emma east?

When Emma left her homestead, Ed moved her shack and joined it to ours to make a bedroom. We nearly froze in it that winter, but the next spring Ed plowed sod and put around it to make it warmer.

What a good feeling it was to walk into my little house and put Nora Julian in the basket that had been fixed up for her, a plain wicker clothes basket covered with cloth and with an overskirt of sheer material. The house was cozy and warm. The teakettle was steaming on the wood range. Ah, how many boilers full of water I heated on that stove, filling them from the barrel that stood on the stone boat outside the door, where it had been hauled from a dam.

A baby in the house certainly made life different. Wonderful, yes, but often worrisome.

By this time, Ed had acquired a saddle horse. If he was out working with the team of mules, it was up to me to water the horse. Rather than haul all that water, I would ride the horse to the dam Ed had built, a quarter of a mile from the house. It usually took me only ten minutes or so. On this one morning, I fastened Nora securely in the little swing we had suspended from the ceiling, then jumped on the horse and headed for the dam. Just before we reached it, the

John Haddy and Ed Hought: proud fathers of new daughters.

horse stopped abruptly. I slid right over his head and landed at the edge of the dam, hurting myself painfully. The horse wheeled and ran home.

As I limped home, I thought I could see someone peeking over the high stone fence that lay just beyond the house. They would look up, then duck down. Could it be Indians? They were too much in the shadow for me to see plainly, but I was terrified. What if they had my little girl? Suddenly I saw a man walking quickly from the barn to the house. I started to run, pain and all. Then I saw it was Leonard Nelson, one of our neighbors.

"Anna," he cried, "where have you been? I've been looking all over for you. I looked in and your little girl was asleep in the swing. I looked in the barn—I was afraid you'd been kicked or thrown into the manger by the horse or one of the cattle. I was planning to take the baby home with me and come back and look some more."

Anna and Nora.

What if he had, and what if I had come home and found the swing empty? And what was it peeking over the fence? Some wild horses that roamed the prairie. They had stopped to graze on the new grass by the stone fence and from time to time would lift their heads to look around.

The wild range horses figured in another frightening episode with Nora. As a baby she slept in a basket on the kitchen table. One night range horses kicked in the kitchen window and glass flew all over Nora—and everywhere. How it scared us! But Nora slept through it all. I remember another time those wild range horses had frightened me. It was in one of my first months in my own shack, and I woke one night to a creaking and scraping in the walls. I was sure some sheepherder was trying to move the shack—with me in it. But it was the horses rubbing up against the rough boards.

Anna with her cousin Oscar.

With a little one to feed, I planted an even larger garden. But the ground was so hard and the summers so hot and dry. One year when Nora was two or three, I had a long row of beans. One bean bush looked better than the rest, but it, too, needed water. "Oh, if only it would rain," I said. "That bush needs water so!"

Nora heard me and trotted over and squatted beside the bush. She was going to take care of that!

One day when Nora was playing in the yard, I heard her scream. My first thought was "rattlesnake!" (John had once killed seven of them on his farm.) But it was no bite—she had sat on a cactus plant. Ed wasn't home, so the hired man held her and I pulled the stickers out.

Then there was Nora and the turkeys. We had never tried to raise turkeys, but one day our hired man got seven turkey eggs from his sister's flock and brought them home to me on horseback, carrying

Nora watching the branding by the sod barn.

them in a pail. I put them under a setting hen and all seven hatched out. What good eating this would be, come winter! But one day there was a heavy, gully-washing rain. It left deep puddles all over. Nora came in. "Mamma, I gave the baby turkeys a bath."

I ran outside. Trying to be helpful, she had washed all seven in a mud puddle and laid them out to dry. There they lay on the sagebrush like dead, six na-ked little creatures. I gathered them up in my apron—maybe I could save them yet!

But six? There should have been seven. Nora pointed her finger. She had dropped the seventh one down through the hole in the outdoor toilet.

Would you believe we saved them all?

Getting the right foods for good nutrition was a problem. Fresh meat in the summer time was one of the hardest needs to cope with. Ed often shot and brought home a sage hen. But sometimes we got so hungry for "real" meat.

One morning shortly after we were married, Ed went to the barn to milk the cow. Suddenly he came running in and, without a word, grabbed his rifle and ran back out.

I hadn't known Ed too well by then. Did he perhaps have a violent temper? Had the cow kicked him? Was he going to shoot the cow in a fit of anger? Oh, dear God, don't let him shoot the cow!

Suddenly I saw a beautiful antelope walk out just beyond the barn wall. "Oh, dear God, don't let him shoot that lovely creature!"

Bang! I heard the gun go off. But the antelope bounded off toward the coulee. "Thank you, God," I breathed.

But it was a long time before Ed returned to the house. When he did, he just put his head in the door and said, "Bring the dishpan." I knew he had followed the antelope and had shot it and was now ready to dress it out.

What mixed feelings I had. I knew we needed the meat, but, oh, what a beautiful creature that had been!

Ed brought the meat home and cut off one of the quarters for a roast. He built a tripod and hung the rest to cure. I fixed the roast for supper that night and I thought it was the most delicious meat I had ever tasted. That night I lay awake for a long time. I thought about the graceful creature running off toward the coulee. Then I thought of the meat we had eaten for supper. The more I thought, the hungrier I grew. At last I got up, went downstairs and cut off a slice of the cold antelope roast.

"Ed," I called upstairs, "come down and eat some meat!" And there we were in the middle of the night, standing around eating this wonderful cold roast.

The cows were our good providers. I made my

own round cheeses. I put rennet tablets in a large pan of milk and warmed it on the back of the stove until the curds and the whey separated. I made a strainer from a three-pound coffee can, with holes punched from the inside. The whey would run off through the holes and the solids would be left in the can. These I emptied into a cheesecloth, tied it up and put it back in the can. I put something heavy on top to weight it down and would even set my sewing machine on top of the other weight to really force out all the liquid.

The whey, too, was cooked down (all day) to make *primost*, adding a little sugar and stirring it until it got thick and brown.

Ed and his friends sometimes went to the Nelson Reservoir to fish for whitefish and buffalo fish. What a treat they were! He brought home many and when I canned them they were as good as any canned salmon.

As I mentioned, Ed often shot sage hens. They are a large bird, with more breast meat than even a pheasant or a quail, but with a strong taste of sage, on which they feed. Soaking them in vinegar and salt water helped remove the wild taste. And I discovered a good way to fix them. We had salted pork down in crocks, but I didn't like it. So when we got a sage hen, I would grind the breast meat and then grind some salt pork, then mix the two together with pepper and spices to make meatballs or meat loaf.

Foodwise, maybe I was ahead of my time that one year.

Ed had decided he would try planting a small field to soybeans. They were quite a novelty at the time. He had bought twenty-five pounds of beans for seed and had put them to soak in a tub so they would germinate sooner. But he had to go off and help a neighbor fix his car. "I'll be back in a couple of hours," he said, and told me to watch the beans.

When he returned, the soybeans had all split in

half. "Why didn't you take them out?" Ed wanted to know.

"I didn't know when they were ready."

"Well, I can throw them all out now."

"No, don't do that. Give them to me."

I cooked and cooked those beans and then I cooked them some more. But they would not get soft. Finally I got my grinder out. I ground them once, then twice, very fine. I took a portion of them and mixed them with chopped onion, salt and pepper and (if I remember right) maybe some bread crumbs. Then I fried them as you would meatballs.

You couldn't tell them from real meatballs! Ed wiped his mouth and grinned. "Now, you ought to send this idea to a newspaper somewhere!"

About that time one of our neighbors stopped in around noontime. "You'd better stay for dinner," Ed said.

"No, no," he shook his head. We all knew food wasn't plentiful on short notice.

"We're having meatballs," Ed said.

Nobody had meatballs for an everyday meal — and at this time of year! Leonard pulled up a chair. First he took sparingly, then he helped himself to more.

"I don't dare go home and tell my wife I've had meatballs for dinner," said Leonard appreciatively. "I don't know when we had meatballs last."

"Well, Leonard," said Ed, "you didn't have them now either."

Pretty soon everyone knew about my now-famous meatballs. And that was long before it was discovered you could use soybeans for many, many things.

Much of the time we had hired hands to feed. Ed loved his team of mules, Trixie and Maud, even though they kicked him every so often. But often the

Gust Peterson with Trixie and Maud.

work got to be too much for him and he would have to have a hired man. One of them was Gust, a real Swede. Gust loved pancakes and he wanted them for breakfast every day.

Well, I got tired of making pancakes every single day. One morning I had ham and eggs and fried potatoes.

"Vell, Mrs. Hought," said Gust, "no panakaker?"

"No, not this morning."

"Allright, then I go home and make my own panakaker."

"Allright, Gust, you do that." Gust put on his cap and walked out the door.

"Anna, you shouldn't have done that," said Ed. "I just lost my hired man."

"He'll be back when he's hungry." I began clearing the table.

Gust lived in a little shack a few miles away. I could just imagine how much food he had there.

Halfway through the day Ed said, "Should I take food over?"

"No. He'll come when he's hungry."

That night I kept supper on the stove after we were finished. When it was dark the dog, who never had liked Gust, began to bark and crowd up against the screen door. There was Gust.

"Come in, Gust," said Ed. Gust rubbed his hands uneasily. "Sit down, Gust."

Gust sat down. I put out dishes and silver and put the rest of supper out. Gust ate a big meal. From that day on, he was a different man. He was always pleasant and polite and I had the feeling he really loved me as a friend. Eventually he moved his shack in to a lot in Malta and fixed it up.

Some of those bachelors who were trying to make it on a homestead had a rough time. I hadn't been in Montana long when Axel Johnson, one of the men living alone, came to my place on skis in winter. He was carrying a sack of flour on his back.

"Anna, I can't make a decent loaf of bread. Will you bake bread for me?"

"Yes, but you really didn't have to bring a whole sack of flour."

"Well," Axel admitted hesitantly, "I wanted you to make it more than once."

And I did. I baked four loaves at a time for him for a long time. Gold or silver wouldn't have been a more welcome gift to him.

Axel later married a girl of seventeen. One day he came on horseback. He was distraught. His young wife had had a miscarriage and he didn't know what to do for her. Neither did I, to be truthful, but I put Nora in the baby carriage and wheeled her across the prairie to Axel's place, about a mile and a half away. What I did in caring for her I did "by guess," but all went well. They later had a fine son, Axel Junior, whom I count among my good friends.

It was not easy for a young wife to adjust to home-steading life, with little or no money. Axel was going to town one day and his wife, Adeline, had made out a list of food she wanted him to pick up. Such a long list she had! Fruit, and things for the baby, and all the good things she missed. But when she counted their money, one thing after another was crossed off. At last there were only four items left: flour, sugar, coffee and snuff. Yes, grocery lists were short.

I tried to show them how to make do with what was at hand. I told Axel he must shoot a sage hen, soak the breast in vinegar water and salt and grind the meat. I showed him other things. In Norway we had cooked nettles for the pigs; in Montana I cooked pigweed. I even cooked nightshade berries. I had always heard they were poisonous (and certainly would not advise anyone else to use them) but an old lady told me she had eaten them all her life. One year I canned forty pints.

Another bachelor, who you might say was a little "simple," told me how tired he was of baking powder biscuits, which were a sort of bachelor staple.

"I have all this oatmeal in a sack," he said. "If only you could bake some bread for me using that oatmeal."

I went over to his place and mixed up a starter, leaving it to bubble up. When I came back to mix up the dough, the starter was doing more than bubble. The oatmeal had been full of worms.

"I thought it looked a little suspicious," said the bachelor sadly, "but I couldn't afford to throw it out."

"Throw it out," I told him. "I'll bake you some bread without oatmeal."

This was a man who later took to drinking a lot. I'm not sure what happened to him.

Contrary to impressions given by books and movies, there was not a great deal of drinking among the homesteaders, or even among the cowboys in that area. A "cowboy" might be one who floated from one farm to another but who preferred working with cattle — and riding a good horse. Or the cowboy might be married and have a shack of his own and would get by picking up small jobs wherever he could find them.

We got mail only when someone had time to ride over to get it. The post office was at Content, about thirteen miles away, a little closer cross-country by horseback. Twice a week, Monday and Friday, the stage brought the mail from Malta. About a mile beyond the post office was the Content Mercantile, as I believe it was called. You could buy a little of everything there. It was run by Ella and Clarence Arneson. Their niece, Carol Kroeger, lived with them, for her mother had passed away. Carol was a bright, charming redhead a few years older than Nora, who adored her. In early homestead days, before so many left that country, they used to hold occasional church services there. Traveling evangelists would come; it was such a man who baptized Nora.

Many people have asked me, how could you live on the desolate prairie after you had grown up in Norway with mountains and hills and trees and beautiful Drammen fjord? There wasn't a single tree in sight of our farm, nor even a large rock. And even when Ed built a dam to hold water for watering the stock, it was a very small body of water.

But it was home. It was MY home. My husband and my baby daughter were here, and I was happy and I wanted to make life as nice as I could.

And there is much that is beautiful about the prairie. The grass waves in the wind like waves of water, and so does the grain as it nears ripening. Sunrise and sunset are things of beauty. Even the winter, which could have treacherous blizzards, was made more bearable by the sudden chinooks, those warm, thawing winds that are so familiar to Montana people.

Sometimes the womenfolk around Content would gather for an afternoon by a creek where there were a few trees. "Everyone brought food and we sat on the ground and had a good visit." Anna and Nora are second from left.

A few years after we were married, Signe, an old friend of mine from Oslo, came to visit me. She was now a personal maid to Mrs. John D. Rockefeller in New York and was used to elegance and fine things. When she first saw our house on the stretch of prairie, she exclaimed, "Oh, Anna, Anna, how can you live in a Sahara like this?" Two weeks later, when it came time for her to say goodbye, she didn't want to leave. She had fallen in love with the prairie, and if she could have found a way she would have settled there for good.

As for the loneliness, we got used to our neighbors being a distance away. Anyone living within fifteen miles we called neighbors. There was actually a lot of social life on the prairie. Many's the time I'd just bake up a cake and send word to a few of the neighbors to come for a visit. Or they might just drop in. We'd sit around and tell stories or talk of what was going on in the neighborhood. Those who were Norwegian liked to keep up on reading *Decorah Posten*, a Norwegian-language paper that came every week, and these were passed on. With some of the settlers we talked Norwegian, with others English, and sometimes it became a mix of both. There were several

Swedish people in the community, also some Scots and Germans, so Content became something of a melting pot.

Sometimes when you invited company you got more than you bargained for. The Hockerts lived fifteen miles away, and one year we invited them to come for Thanksgiving dinner. We had our own turkey that fall, and the day before Thanksgiving I was in the middle of cleaning it.

Suddenly Nora called, "Somebody's coming!"

"Can you see who it is?"

"Well, it's the Hockerts' horses, I can see that."

"Goodness, am I mixed up? Is it Thanksgiving today? No, of course not, it's tomorrow."

The Hockerts pulled up by the barn, ready to put the horses away. They came tromping up to the house, shaking the snow off their heavy horsehair coats. I opened the door.

"Happy Thanksgiving!" they cried.

I picked up the courage to say, "Did you think it was today?"

"Oh, no, we knew it was tomorrow but we came today so we could stay longer."

I finished cleaning the turkey. They stayed overnight and we enjoyed our dinner together. Finally, by late afternoon, I had to ask, "When are you planning to go home and do your chores?"

"Oh, we turned the calf loose, so that will take care of the milking. And we shoveled snow into the chicken pen so they can eat snow if their water freezes up."

We played whist far into the night and whenever we weren't stuffing ourselves with Thanksgiving food, we laughed and joked and had a wonderful time. After they got home, they sent us a letter telling us everything was fine at home. The chickens were laying eggs and the calf had taken care of the milking.

It was at Hockerts' farm that we spent a memorable Fourth of July, one of those Fourths where the corn was knee-high as it was supposed to be. Unless farm work was too pressing, we usually celebrated the Fourth in some way with others in the community. This year the Hockerts had built a dance floor and we were going to have a dance to initiate it. Lots of people turned out for it, all bringing food, and the Hockerts and their two little girls welcomed us.

But we hadn't been there long when a black storm cloud moved over the sky and a terrible storm broke loose. People hid under cars and buggies as the hail came pelting down. Wind and hail knocked out all the windows on one side of the farmhouse.

"There won't be a stalk of corn left in the fields," said Ed. When we drove home we saw that field after field was stripped bare. I had set three hens on eggs in nests out in the yard. I never saw a sign of them again—hens, eggs, all were gone. I often wondered what happened to them.

Drought, hail, wind all took their toll. Even wild animals were a worry. One early Sunday morning, when everything was still, the dog began to bark. There in the yard were two coyotes, each with a turkey in its mouth. Ed fired his shotgun and one dropped his turkey and ran. "They had enough with one," shrugged Ed.

Ed worked hard, so very hard. There was always so much to do and it seemed like there was never enough time to do it. He was in the fields, or out picking rocks, or sometimes exchanging work with a neighbor. I was often alone, which meant I had to handle chores around the place.

One day I had finished a particularly big washing. I had washed all the downstairs curtains and had hung everything on the line. Then it was time to go feed the newborn calf some milk. As I came up the incline from the barn, I glanced toward the clothesline to admire my nice white washing. But it was all on the ground! All forty pigs had gotten loose, and they had grabbed at clothes they could reach and pulled the lines down. There had been a rain the day before, and they were wallowing in the mud, ripping my beautiful curtains apart, together with the only white shirt Ed owned. I walked into the house and lay down and cried.

Another day, when I was very pregnant with Nora, my neighbor came over and found me lying on the ground.

"Anna, are you allright?"

"I'm allright," I said, raising myself up. "I've just been chasing pigs."

But as hard as I worked, I am sure Ed worked harder, even though he had come home from the war with only one lung and had been warned to be careful. We had an old truck with solid rubber tires that almost pounded us to death as we jolted over the prairie and through the coulees on roads that were next to no roads. One year, just before spring work started, Ed was cranking the truck and it "kicked," breaking his arm. Can you imagine how hard it was, catching, feeding and harnessing several head of horses, hitching them to the machinery and putting in a full day's work in the field — with a broken arm?

Not long after Nora was born, the government decided that it should do something more for its veterans who had been wounded during the war. Ed was offered a chance to attend the Agricultural College at Montana State University in Bozeman. We moved there and settled into a tiny apartment, and it was here that our second daughter, Mary Elaine, was born on Christmas Eve, 1922. "A beautiful child," the doctor said.

A heart condition that had started at Nora's birth

had worsened, and I was very ill after Mary Elaine was born. It seemed to be one thing after another, and the doctor said I could not get up. All I could manage to eat was a little milk toast.

The lady downstairs, Mrs. Floor, gave the baby a bath morning and evening. Ed hired a woman to come and care for us, but she did nothing but rock in the rocking chair. "Ed," I said, "she's no good, she doesn't do anything." But Ed said, "Well, she's sitting here anyway." It was he who had to do the washing, cooking, housekeeping and taking care of Nora, who was then two and a half—and he was going to school as well.

At last I recovered enough so we could return to Content and the farm. But on the train trip back both Nora and the baby developed pneumonia. By the time we reached Malta, Mary Elaine was so ill we had to put her in the hospital. It's like a nightmare, as if I could barely think at the time. The doctor we had known was away. A nurse was running the hospital. The doctor who tended the baby said, "Don't put a hot water bottle on." But the nurse said to me later, "He doesn't know as much about this as I do," and she put a hot water bottle on that burned the baby's chest. One thing led to another. At last we saw the little life ebb out.

A nurse gave me a shot to make me sleep. But suddenly someone was shaking me and saying, "Mrs. Hought, your baby is alive! Come!"

Weak and dizzy, I followed her. In her little basket Mary Elaine opened her eyes, gave a cry, and died. It was the morning of Easter Sunday.

There was the funeral to see to. Neighbors at the farm offered to take care of Nora, so Ed brought her out to them for a couple of days. On one night they took her with them to a local dance. They made a bed for her on the floor in a corner and covered her with coats to keep her warm. But as the evening wore on, others came and, seeing the pile of coats, piled their sheepskins on top of it. A friend of ours told us later, "I finally realized Nora was under there. I dug her out and held her on my knee. She clung to me as if she knew me. I thought, 'What would Anna say if she knew?' " God bless his memory.

Perhaps the hardest of all was coming home after the funeral and having Nora ask, "Where is my baby sister?" Oh, how that hurt! I said, "You don't have a baby sister now."

"But where is she?"

"We will see her again some day."

But for a long time after that Nora would look under the bed and in all the corners, searching for her baby sister.

When we went into town early in the summer, I brought flowers for Mary Elaine's grave. But when we found the grave marked as hers, I said, "This isn't the right grave."

"How do you know?" asked Ed.

"I know. I just don't feel right about it."

Ed had to go find the man in charge of the cemetery. He looked up the records, and sure enough, this was the grave of an old person. When he pointed out the correct grave I felt at peace.

There were other heartaches. My father died. Then, at one point I had not heard from my mother for about five months. I thought it strange, for she used to write as soon as she got my letters, but mail at that time was very slow. Then one day in a letter from my brother George, he wrote, "Wasn't it terrible that Mother died?" It was the first I knew, and it had been many months! Oscar's wife in Norway had written the address as "Cont." instead of "Mont." and the letter had finally come back to them marked "address unknown." I remember that Nora came and put her arms around me. "Oh, Mamma," she said, "I'm so sorry."

Heartache was part of life for many in the new land. My cousin Ragna married Christian Andreason, a fine young man, in Norway. He came to America, to Chicago. He went back for Ragna and their son, who had been born after Christian left for America. On the ship Christian became ill. It turned out he had tuberculosis. He was sick for a long time and unable to work. Ragna didn't know the language. She took in washing and would spend long days at the wash board, often with a sick baby on her shoulder. Christian died, then their little boy, and then the little girl who was born after they came to Chicago.

Many years later I was able to get Ragna's address. She had just lost her second husband and was recovering from two major surgeries, and was so despondent. I invited her to visit us, and with good food, good stories, laughter and love she was soon in good health again.

The heart problem plagued me for many years in Montana. It started with my first pregnancy. Pregnancy and delivery at that age is difficult, and our diet was certainly lacking. No fresh meat was available for weeks at a time (only salt pork, greasy, packed in smelly brine), no fresh fruits and vegetables (and how I missed all those I had come to know working in Great Falls). Then, in my early forties my hair suddenly began to turn gray, and then turned snow white. I was not well at all. Finally we went to a doctor in Great Falls, who diagnosed it as pernicious anemia and told me I would have to eat liver every day. Well, imagine how difficult it was to have fresh liver every day, living thirty-five miles from town and having no kind of refrigeration! But about that time liver extract became available and, miracle of miracles, the anemia was cured.

But the heart spells continued and got progressively worse. When the pain came, I suffered terribly. I couldn't lie down in bed; I would have to keep my head out and one foot in, one out of bed. Sometimes I could lie and look at one thing on the wall for a long time, and suddenly the pain would stop, like turning off a switch. Poor Ed would ask people to look in on me. Once Axel Johnson and another neighbor sat by my bed and cried, they were so sure I was going to die. It wasn't until years later that a doctor prescribed digitalis, and the spells ended.

But life went on. We took things as they came and made the best of it. There was, for instance, the neighbor lady who was such a good sport about everything. She told us all about how she had her baby at home. Her husband was out putting machinery together when she called him and said, "It's time!" He came running in and didn't take time to wash, for the baby was about there. When it was out, she said, "Take some white thread and tie off the cord." There was no thought of sterilization. The thread got wet. "Dry it off," she told him, and he ran it through his dirty fingers and wiped his hands on his overalls. She laughed as she told us about it.

But the worry and isolation proved to be too great a burden for some. When the Hovey family had a new baby, I suggested to Ed one Sunday that we take a ride to see them. Mrs. Hovey was still in bed, but a nurse was there caring for her. The nurse was also doing the cooking, and Mrs. Hovey insisted that we stay for lunch. We sat at the table—Mr. Hovey, Ed, Nora and myself. I'm not sure where the rest of the Hovey children were.

In the middle of lunch, Hovey got up and went out of the door like a shot. From her bed his wife said, "Maybe he's having one of his funny spells." We were uncomfortable and decided to leave. When we came outside, he was lying in the yard. We thanked him for lunch. "Oh, that's nothing," he replied and we said goodbye. On our way home Ed and I talked about his strange behavior. "Do you suppose he doesn't like us?" I wondered.

By the next weekend Ed had to go to town with a load of wheat. I stayed home as I had invited company for Sunday. But by Saturday evening Ed still hadn't returned from town. Sunday morning Nora and I were still upstairs when I heard a neighbor call,

"Anna, Anna, are you allright? This is Christine, are you allright?"

I hurried downstairs. "We were worried," said Christine. "Nels Simonson was up here earlier and your storm door was blowing in the wind. He opened the door and looked in. Your clothes were on the chair but he didn't see you anywhere and we were afraid something had happened."

"But why? Has something happened to Ed?"

"No. But Hovey went berserk this morning and killed his wife and the baby and the two-year-old girl. He was going to kill the boys, too, but they managed to roll under the barbed-wire fence and ran to the neighbors."

My knees almost buckled under me. By noon some of the neighbors came, but Ed still wasn't home. A little past noon he came with the horses and wagon. He came in and sat down at the table and put his head in his hands. Soon after a man came riding up.

"They've found Hovey," he announced. "Found him in the granary. He'd shot himself."

I remember I dropped the platter of meat on the table.

A year or two after that we had an old truck and had to go to one of the neighbors, the Kjos farm, on an errand. As we came through the coulee near the old Hovey place, the truck stopped. Ed had to go back to the Kjos's to get a lantern. Nora and I sat in the pitch blackness and waited. How spooky it was! I could imagine Hovey walking back and forth between his buildings.

"Mamma, are you scared?"

"No, Nora."

"I am."

Ed got the truck started and we headed home. But of all the places in the neighborhood, it was one I would have picked in which NOT to wait in the dark.

Many strange things happened. I was home alone one day when the dog began barking. Ed was away helping a neighbor. I saw a car with two men in it pull into our yard. I was uneasy as one of them started for our door. The dog growled and crouched against the screen door.

"What can I do for you?" I asked.

"Well, I have a crazy man in the car."

"How do you know he's crazy?"

"I'm trying to take him home but he doesn't know where he lives. All he can say is that when he left home the door was in the north but now it's gone." The man laughed and laughed. The man in the car laughed, too, and made faces.

"Well, he can't stay here."

"Are you alone?"

"Yes, but my husband will be home any minute," I said quickly. "But there's no room here."

"Well, we sure don't want him."

"Go a little further down the road, someone will help out."

Later we heard that the man in question had put his mother in a hayrack, then whipped the horses. She had gone down the trail screaming until at last she fell off.

Sometimes acquaintances or even strangers would get caught out on the prairie as darkness fell and would seek shelter for the night. Some had traveled all through the West and had strange stories to tell. One man who spent the night told of coming to one place in winter. He called out, "Anyone home?" and was answered with a roar—but could not see anyone in the room. Then he looked up. There above the hot stove was a chair tied to the rafters. In it sat a man trying to get warm.

But never did we have as much company as we did the year we first acquired a radio! It was 1927, and we had sold some wheat. Ed gave me a choice—a radio or a washing machine. Since I really didn't think a machine would get my clothes as clean as I could on my own scrub board, I chose the radio. It must have been one of the first around, for neighbors came from all directions to listen to it in the evenings. How they laughed, listened and wondered and talked about what they were hearing. We laughed over Amos and Andy, but from the beginning the prize fights were the favorites among the men.

The radio had headphones, so everyone had to take turns listening. It squeaked and squawked. One would just get interested in a broadcast and then— SQUAWK! It was an undependable connection with an almost foreign world—Omaha, Denver, Salt Lake City. Then the batteries would run down—A batteries, B's and C's. And who had money for more?

The trouble with having a radio was that everyone came to listen in the evening. Then it was too dark to go home by horseback or wagon, so I had to feed them all around midnight and then they stayed overnight. And I gave them breakfast in the morning! We had a hired man named Cleveland who got downright disgusted with all the people who came and wouldn't go home.

By this time we had accumulated a few head of cattle and from time to time we would sell some to get money for things we needed or wanted. The same

Nora scraping the frosting bowl.

year we got the radio, we also got carbide lights. The carbide powered not only the lights, but also a wonderful three-burner stove and even an iron, just like an electric iron. It ironed clothes perfectly. We had to buy large cans of carbide and keep them outside to power it all.

Nora was seven. When she first saw the lights, she cried, "Oh, Mamma, it looks like a Christmas tree!"

Nora started school. We traded a young horse to Hugh Miller for Old Henry, a retired roping horse. He took Nora the three miles to school for a few years. Ed hung a ring in a long strap beside the stirrup so she could put her right foot in that and her left foot in the stirrup in order to climb into the saddle.

Between our place and Washington School were

Nora and neighbor Ed Ferm.

three gates that had to be opened and closed morning and afternoon, so she made many a climb up and down that stirrup. At the school was a barn where the children's horses were stabled during the day. Fathers took turns bringing hay.

One winter, midway through a school day, one of those sudden and vicious Montana blizzards started up. The John Haddys and Leonard Nelsons lived nearest the school. John Haddy quickly hitched his team to the sled, drove to the Nelsons' and picked Leonard up and came to the school. The teacher dismissed the pupils early. John sent Leonard home with his team and with the Haddy and Nelson children. Then John mounted Old Henry and, putting Nora behind him to shelter her from the wind, started for our place.

Meanwhile, I was begging Ed to hitch up the team and go look for Nora. He said it would be useless and dangerous because the way the snow was blowing they could pass each other and never know it. Finally, when it seemed to let up a little, he started out. And that is exactly what happened—they passed in the storm and would not have seen each other. But Nora heard the jingle of the harness and shouted to him, and they found each other.

When they all three came into the house, I was so happy I cried. The Lord had indeed taken care of them all. I told John how I wished I had something to give him.

"Well," he smiled, "I'd be happy to have a piece of that pie!"

One day, when Nora was a little older, a man came by on a beautiful saddle horse. Nora fell in love with that horse, and we learned he was for sale. But was he safe?

"I wouldn't sell him to your little girl if he wasn't safe, and I wouldn't sell him to anyone but you." And so we bought her beloved Teddy for ninety-five dollars and Old Henry was retired.

Sometimes the winters were long. For a time there was a teacher at Washington School, Miss Kelly, from Williston, North Dakota. She lived at the school and boarded herself and her sister, who had come to stay with her. It was lonely for the two girls, with no car and only catching a ride to town once in a while with some farmer going in on an errand. So we parents tried to make it a little more interesting for them. Sometimes we'd plan a picnic, or some wintertime get-togethers where everyone brought something to eat. Or we might pool our money and buy about three gallons of oysters for a stew, with lots of good milk and cream and floating in butter.

There was one Christmas party when the teachers had decorated the little one-room school so beautifully, even making a make-believe fireplace. Curtis Nelson was dressed as Santa Claus. He was to come down the chimney and out of the fireplace with a sack of gifts, which he would put under the tree.

But Curtis's whiskers caught fire from the candles on the tree. Poor Curtis was burning and there was a rush as people tried to put out the fire on him and the tree, which was also afire. Women with their little ones were crowding to get into the hallway and out through the only outside door. The men by then were outside working on Curtis, putting wagon grease on his sores.

I put my little girl on a table next to a window, thinking that rather than fighting to get out I would send her out the window if the fire got the upper hand, and I could help others through, too. But the fire was finally brought under control.

For days afterward Nora went around the house saying, "Too bad, too bad. Santa Claus got hurt and Curtis Nelson got burned, too!"

When the time came for Nora to start high school in Malta, thirty-five miles away, there was nothing to do but to rent a housekeeping room where she could stay for the next four terms. She didn't want to go in by herself, so we picked up our favorite cat, Sugar, and the two of us went in. At Herschmans the room was ready for us with a bed, a table, two chairs, a three-burner gas plate and an oven for it, which I had brought from home. (The oven I used to store cookies in).

Soon I had to get a few more things—a dresser, a couple more chairs. What we were not happy about was that the rubber hose from the bottled gas tanks to the burners looked terribly unsafe. We were afraid if we bumped it it might come loose and leak gas. And I know Ed at home worried about it.

And we worried about him. He had about fifty head of cattle to feed and water every day. Every day in the winter he had to chop open the frozen waterhole on the dam. At times the animals were so thirsty they couldn't wait, and they pushed him and bumped him until he could hardly get water to them. He felt like giving up. Then a neighbor from three miles away who had a running spring offered him all the water he needed if he would drive the cattle back and forth. It was a lifesaver, but think of the work getting them back and forth.

But then came the chinook winds. The snow melted and there was water all over—praise the Lord! We knew it in town, too, for we had felt the warm winds. Ed came in to town. We slept three in the bed that night—four counting the cat, who had a place on her own blanket at the foot of the bed.

I went back out with him that time as it was time to butcher. I canned a beef, churned butter, baked bread, cleaned the house, made pies and cakes, all in one week. Other times I sent out bread and other things with neighbors who came to town and stopped to see us.

Nora was sick a lot during that year, and I was glad I was there to care for her. But there was too, much work on the farm to leave Ed alone, and the next school year Nora stayed with others.

Not only the work, but the terrible drought of those years made this a hard time to struggle through.

Beyond The Prairie

The depression years of the 1930s were difficult years for the whole country. But what many forget is that in Montana there were several drought years in a row, on top of the Depression. Year after year we got back barely enough grain for seed for the next year; many failed even to get back that much. Things finally became so bad that some people were practically starving.

"Ed," I would say, "leave the seed in the granary, don't bother to plant. All you get back is seed for another year, that is all."

"No," Ed would say, "that's not right. The Lord means for us to at least try."

And try we did. We had built up a fair herd of cattle and sometimes we could ship one and get back a little money. But by 1935 the rains still had not come and even the pastures were drying up. We were forced to cut expenses to the point where we didn't even eat the proper foods. It seemed that the only thing we could do was to sell our cattle, which we did. Cattle prices at that time were fairly good; by the next year they had dropped so low that some farmers were left with only a shipping bill to pay.

John and Loraine had decided to try to stick it out, and we sold my homestead to John for $1,000. If I had to part with my hard-earned land, I was glad for John to have it. The government bought Ed's land.

In 1935, we bought a lot in Malta. On it was a barn but no house. At about this time Ed's brother was leaving his homestead, so we bought his house and moved it onto our lot. Our own farmhouse we sold to the family who owned the funeral parlor in Malta; they moved it into town and added it to their house.

Ed's brother Elmer was a shipper of cattle from all over the country. When Ed shipped our cattle to South St. Paul, he went to Alexandria, near the area where his parents had lived. Seeing his wide-brimmed hat and boots, a man on the street remarked, "You must be a Montana cowboy."

"No," said Ed, explaining how he had come to sell out in the terrible dry years. Then he asked, "Are there any large farms for sale around here?"

"I might know of just what you want," answered the man.

Ed went out and looked over the farm in question. When he came home that time, he said, "Well, I bought a farm in Minnesota."

"Oh, no! Without me seeing it?"

"Yes." But Ed was smiling.

"But that's not fair!" I protested.

Then it came out. Ed was teasing me. He hadn't bought it. "But you and I are going back to look at it."

We found a farm with lots of grass and with springs from which came plenty of water. How good that water looked after our dried-up crops. There was a good pump, too, and good drinking water. We bought the farm and moved the few head of cattle we had with which to start a new herd.

One of the delightful features of the farm was a small lake, which would come to be a real benefit to the livestock. But when we moved there, Minnesota was also suffering from the drought and the lake was dry. So dry, in fact, that Ed and his relatives hunted pheasants in the lake bottom.

The barn was big, the biggest one around there. The house was an old log building with neither water nor electricity. On the main floor was a living room, kitchen and bedroom, and upstairs were two more bedrooms. The kitchen was an old-fashioned one, with a stairway leading upstairs right behind the stove. Old Uncle Beckstrom came to straighten out that stairway, which was an improvement.

Our first look at the inside of the house was a shock. It was filthy. The upstairs had been used as a chicken coop! The place had been sold by Anton Pederson to a dealer in Osakis, who had rented it out for ten years before we bought it. We had not been able to see the inside of the house before we bought it—the renter didn't want us to.

"Oh, if only Ray Bondy was here!" I cried. Ray had worked for us in Montana and had later moved to Minnesota. In the next day or two, who should come to visit but Ray Bondy!

"I heard you'd moved to Minnesota and I thought I'd see if you needed some help," said Ray.

"Yes, right away," Ed responded.

"Well, I'm ready right now."

The next day Ray and I started on the upstairs. He scrubbed and I rinsed and rinsed, changed water and changed water. In time it smelled like a hospital and we were beginning to be able to see the floor.

The next day we started on the downstairs bedroom and it was almost as bad. Beside the dirt, we

made another unpleasant discovery—bedbugs! So I
went to stay with some relatives for awhile while Ed
and Uncle Beckstrom fumigated and plastered in
places where it was needed.

"You needn't do a good job in there," Ed told
me, "you'll never get me to sleep in there anyway!"

But Ray and I scrubbed and scrubbed. We
painted walls and ceiling, put in window panes where
they were missing and hung nice curtains. I laid down
the new rugs I had braided in Malta and brought in
my bedroom set and cedar chest.

"Come and look," I called to Ed at last. "Will
you sleep in here tonight?"

"Don't see why not," said a surprised Ed. "It
really looks nice."

With the whole house finally cleaned up and
looking nice and cozy, it was time to start on the outside. One day I was out chopping ice and chicken ma-
nure in the yard when two young men passed by at a
distance, heading for the lake to fish. I was wearing an
old black felt hat to keep warm. Later I learned the
boys had gone home and told their mother they had
seen the new lady on the next farm.

"What does she look like?"

"She's real dark," reported the boys, "and she
works real hard outside."

"Oh," said their mother, "I'm sure she is a hard-
working German woman."

After three months, they came to call—Ida
and Anton Pederson and Anton's brother Christian,
who had a farm on the other side of Anton's. When
they came to the door and asked if I was the lady of the
house, they could hardly believe it—me with snow
white hair and absolutely Scandinavian! They told
me what their boys had said and we had a good laugh.
Ida and her daughter were to become good friends of
mine.

We quickly got acquainted with more people and soon joined the First Lutheran Church of Osakis, whose pastor was Rev. Carmen Thronson. After some time, Rev. Thronson also preached at Nelson, and since that was closer to our home, we joined there. Pastor Thronson had previously served near Malta, but we didn't know them then.

Meanwhile, Ed had built a chicken house, hog house, machine shed and later a silo. He improved the looks of the farmstead and with the Herefords we had managed to save from Montana we started out with cattle again.

But the work proved to be too much for Ed, and after four and a half years he suffered a stroke. The doctor gave orders that he was to quit farming. We rented out the farm and moved to Nelson. (We had two renters on the place and eventually our daughter Nora and her husband, Marlin Hoglund, took over the place.)

So we moved into Nelson, a small town outside Alexandria. Here we rented the main floor of Otto Larson's house. Otto's wife had passed away and he and his two daughters, Ethel and Inez, lived upstairs; but both the girls were working in Minneapolis then. What a pleasant place it was, and how close I felt to the two girls, almost like a mother. To this day they call me "Tante Anna."

Ed, who liked carpentry and was anxious for something to do, found an old home close to the Lutheran Church which needed work and we bought it. But while he was still remodeling, we had a chance to rent a lovely new house that had belonged to the owner of the elevator in town. There had been an explosion at the elevator and the owner had been killed. His wife came to me and said, "Anna, I want you to rent my home and I will let you have it cheap." She was

After the prairie: Anna and Ed Hought.

a teacher and planned now to return to teaching and felt she wanted to live in a smaller home. So, while we hated to leave the Larsons, we took it. Then in two years our home was ready and we moved into that.

Those years in Nelson, with many things going on, were pleasant indeed. One of my memories is of cooking rommegrot for church suppers, often for as many as five hundred people. I would cook it at home, using my own kettles and my "stirrer," and when it was finished we would pour it into an electric roaster to keep it warm and bring it to the church. But we never covered it — somehow it changed the taste if it was allowed to stand covered.

The summer of 1954 seemed no different from any other, but it was to be one I would never forget.

Ed's brother Elmer, who had also farmed in Montana, had bought a large summer resort near Motley, Minnesota, with many small cabins which he rented out in summer. That year he had promised a cabin to a couple but found he did not have time to build it himself, so Ed would go up a week at a time to help him.

One day, when they had almost finished the cabin, Ed said, "Well, all that's left is to put in one window and you can do that. So I think I'll go home tomorrow."

Then Ed stood looking out over the lake. "Isn't this beautiful?" he remarked. "I think I'll come up here and retire."

A little while later Ed commented that he wasn't feeling well. "I think I'll go up and lie down for a little while." He walked up a small incline, found a grassy spot under an evergreen tree and lay down — and there he died.

Epilogue

Anna Hought has spent the past seventeen years in Seattle, where Nora and Marlin and their children had already settled. For most of that time she had her own apartment; since 1982 she has lived with a granddaughter, Linda Gutzman, in nearby Kent. Anna has three grandchildren and six great-grandchildren: Barbro and Gorman Donithan are the parents of Steve, Julie Ann, and Dylan; Linda and Michael Gutzman's children are Jay and Ron, and Stephen Hoglund's son is Sean.

Anna made two trips back to Norway, and has, well into her nineties, traveled to Washington, D.C., and other places. Not one to live in the past, Anna has friends all over the city who, for several years, came to learn Hardanger embroidery from her. She began teaching at ninety-one and continued for two and a half years. The classes she taught in West Seattle have started several others teaching, and the old Norwegian craft brightens many Northwest homes. She has demonstrated the craft in festivals and classes in the Space Needle, the University of Washington and other places.

Recently Anna wrote the following in one of

her many notebooks:

> I would often go to the Foss Home in Seattle to visit elderly residents. Once when I was there I heard there were two ladies who were a hundred years old. Since I was only ninety-four at the time, I thought I would ask their advice on growing old.
>
> "I came to get your recipe to be 100," I said to the first one. "What did you do these last six years?"
>
> "There is nothing to look forward to," she answered dejectedly. "I just sit here and wait."
>
> "Do you keep busy? Perhaps crochet? Knit?"
> "What for?"
>
> I went to the second one. She was in a wheel chair, but she was happy and smiling. I asked her the same question.
>
> "A recipe? Yes, you shall have it, you shall have it." Then she began to talk about all kinds of things, things that had happened in the past.
>
> Finally I broke in. "I have to go," I said, "but what about the recipe?"
>
> "Oh, yes, the recipe! Let's see, was it for the cake or the cookies?"
>
> So I will have to leave you with my own recipe: Be happy and content. Thank God for all that life brings your way. And always, do for others.

There is an echo of Skoger in her words, and of Oslo, and of early spring days on the prairie when a chinook sent water rushing through the coulees and one knew—oh, surely this year!—the crop would be good.